Access to History

General Editor: Keith Randell

The Early Stuarts 1603-40

Access to History

General Editor: Keith Randell

The Early Stuarts 1603-40

Katherine Brice

Hodder & Stoughton

A MEMBER OF THE HODDER HEADLINE GROUP

The cover illustration shows a portrait of Charles I by Van Dyck (Courtesy of National Portrait Gallery, London)

Some other titles in the series:

Henry VII Caroline Rogers	ISBN 0 340 53801 5
Henry VIII and the Government of England Keith Randell	ISBN 0 340 55325 1
Henry VIII and the Reformation in England Keith Randell	ISBN 0 340 57805 X
Edward VI and Mary: A Mid-Tudor Crisis? Nigel Heard	ISBN 0 340 53560 1
Elizabeth I: Religion and Foreign Affairs John Warren	ISBN 0 340 55518 1
Tudor Economy and Society Nigel Heard	ISBN 0 340 55519 X
The Interregnum 1649-60 Michael Lynch	ISBN 0 340 58207 3

British Library Cataloguing in Publication Data

A catalogue for this book is
available from the British Library
Pearce, Robert

ISBN 0-340-57510-7

First published 1994

Impression number 10   9   8   7   6   5   4   3   2
Year   1998   1997   1996   1995

Typeset by Sempringham publishing, Bedford
Printed in Great Britain for Hodder & Stoughton Educational, a division of Hodder Headline Plc, 338 Euston Road, London NW1 3BH by Page Bros, Norwich.

Contents

Preface

To the general reader

Although the *Access to History* series has been designed with the needs of students studying the subject at higher examination levels very much in mind, it also has a great deal to offer the general reader. The main body of the text (i.e. ignoring the Study Guides at the ends of chapters) forms a readable and yet stimulating survey of a coherent topic as studied by historians. However, each author's aim has not merely been to provide a clear explanation of what happened in the past (to interest and inform): it has also been assumed that most readers wish to be stimulated into thinking further about the topic and to form opinions of their own about the significance of the events that are described and discussed (to be challenged). Thus, although no prior knowledge of the topic is expected on the reader's part, she or he is treated as an intelligent and thinking person throughout. The author tends to share ideas and possibilities with the reader, rather than passing on numbers of so-called 'historical truths'.

To the student reader

There are many ways in which the series can be used by students studying History at a higher level. It will, therefore, be worthwhile thinking about your own study strategy before you start your work on this book. Obviously, your strategy will vary depending on the aim you have in mind, and the time for study that is available to you.

If, for example, you want to acquire a general overview of the topic in the shortest possible time, the following approach will probably be the most effective:

1 Read chapter 1 and think about its contents.
2 Read the 'Making notes' section at the end of chapter 2 and decide whether it is necessary for you to read this chapter.
3 If it is, read the chapter, stopping at each heading to note down the main points that have been made.
4 Repeat stage 2 (and stage 3 where appropriate) for all the other chapters.

If, however, your aim is to gain a thorough grasp of the topic, taking however much time is necessary to do so, you may benefit from carrying out the same procedure with each chapter, as follows:

1 Read the chapter as fast as you can, and preferably at one sitting.
2 Study the flow diagram at the end of the chapter, ensuring that you understand the general 'shape' of what you have just read.

3 Read the 'Making notes' section (and the 'Answering essay questions' section, if there is one) and decide what further work you need to do on the chapter. In particularly important sections of the book, this will involve reading the chapter a second time and stopping at each heading to think about (and to write a summary of) what you have just read.

4 Attempt the 'Source-based questions' section. It will sometimes be sufficient to think through your answers, but additional understanding will often be gained by forcing yourself to write them down.

When you have finished the main chapters of the book, study the 'Further Reading' section and decide what additional reading (if any) you will do on the topic.

This book has been designed to help make your studies both enjoyable and successful. If you can think of ways in which this could have been done more effectively, please write to tell me. In the meantime, I hope that you will gain greatly from your study of History.

Keith Randell

Acknowledgements

The Publishers would like to thank the following for permission to reproduce illustrations in this volume:

Cover - 'Charles I on Horseback' by Anthony Van Dyck, The National Gallery, London; Benjamin Wright/National Portrait Gallery, London p 25; National Portrait Gallery, London p 63, p 81; Department of Prints and Drawings, The British Museum p 105, p 117; The Royal Collection © Her Majesty The Queen p 115.

Every effort has been made to trace and acknowledge ownership of copyright. The Publishers will be glad to make suitable arrangements with any copyright holders whom it has not been possible to contact.

CHAPTER 1

Introduction: Britain, 1603-40

On a chilly morning in January 1649, Charles I, anointed King of England, Wales, Ireland and Scotland, God's representative on earth, was executed in Whitehall. Kings had been deposed, murdered, forced to abdicate or killed in battle but never before or since has a British monarch been tried in an imitation of one of his own courts and condemned to death. This event, probably the single most shocking fact in English constitutional history, and the civil war which preceded it for seven bitter years, have preoccupied historians from that time onwards. This volume looks at the 40 years preceding the outbreak of civil war, from the accession of James I in 1603. In March of that year a courtier galloped north with the news that James had been waiting for. Elizabeth I was dead and with her the Tudor dynasty, and James VI of Scotland was the acknowledged and accepted new sovereign, king by virtue of descent (he was the son of Elizabeth's cousin, Mary Queen of Scots) and because there was no real alternative. It would have been impossible to predict in 1603 that in less than 50 years England would be convulsed by civil war and the monarchy itself abolished.

What went wrong? Was there a series of steps leading progressively and inexorably towards breakdown, which has been called a 'high road to civil war'? Or was it merely a series of blunders by the main participants, above all Charles I, which tipped the scales towards conflict? Was religion, finance, administrative breakdown or class struggle at the root of the problem? Historians have held all these views in an astonishing diversity of interpretations. However, the most recent scholarship sees the civil war as the product of a combination of circumstances that existed and mistakes that were made between 1637 and 1642. The constitution had lost the ability to absorb crises because it was under stress caused above all by an inadequate system of finance, and the strains of the five years from 1637 were enough to bring it to breakdown. While studying the period before the civil war it is important to note what the stresses in government were so that you can understand what happened next, but it is also important to remember that the civil war might never have happened, that it was the last thing that any contemporary would have expected and that the accession of James I brought no structural changes from the reign of Elizabeth I.

The period divides into three. The first covers the years 1603 to 1618. This was a time of conflict between king and parliament, principally over finance but also concerning James's desire for union between England and Scotland. However, apart from these issues, this was a time of stability and underlying harmony. The next period was from 1618 to 1629. The Thirty Years War on the continent increased fears about religion and England's inept foreign policy, and the leadership of the Duke of Buckingham led to serious attacks in the House of Commons on the direction of crown policy. The final period of 1629 to 1640 is known as the personal rule of Charles I because he decided to dispense with parliaments. There was little active opposition during this time, but when parliament met again in 1640 the accumulated grievances of the previous 11 years united virtually the entire political nation against the king.

James I had problems with his parliaments almost from the start. He was extravagant and crown finances were inadequate at the best of times. The king was not always well served by his ministers and his fondness for handsome young men, above all George Villiers, whom he promoted in stages until he became the Duke of Buckingham, caused great resentment. The outbreak of the Thirty Years War which led to the dispossessing of James's daughter Elizabeth and her husband Frederick, the Elector Palatine, created unease about the direction of James's foreign policy and conflict about the financing and conduct of a war.

Despite murmurs about James's plan to marry his son Charles to a Catholic princess - first, unsuccessfully to the Spanish Infanta and then to the French king's sister - there were no serious worries about religion in James's reign. When Charles I came to the throne in 1625 it was a different matter. He rapidly promoted men who attacked the official Calvinist orthodoxy of the Church of England (which included a belief in predestination) and many who were previously in the mainstream of the Church were driven into opposition. Charles maintained the favour shown to the Duke of Buckingham to the virtual exclusion of all other advice. He pursued a disastrous foreign policy involving simultaneous war against the two most powerful European nations, France and Spain. Buckingham was assassinated in 1628, after which the distance between Charles and his subjects increased. When parliament was not prepared to grant the taxes Charles asked for he resolved to rule without it and from 1629 to 1640 he had no meeting with the representatives of his subjects.

The personal rule was brought to an end by Charles's decision to impose the English religious settlement on the Presbyterian Scots. This provoked a national outcry in the land of Charles's birth and he was forced to raise an army which required the summoning of a parliament to finance it. The Short Parliament of March 1640 achieved nothing. The Scots invaded England in the summer and occupied Northumberland and County Durham. Charles was forced to summon another parliament and this time he had to consider its grievances before the MPs would attend to his problems. The unwilling manner in which he made any concessions caused the more radical members of parliament to push for more and more reforms. This alarmed others who switched back to support for the king. Thus two sides emerged and steadily moved into more extreme positions. The attempt by Charles to arrest five MPs by force was a turning point: parliament retreated into the City and Charles turned his back on the capital and sought support elsewhere. With direct communication at an end, the approach of war came steadily and in August 1642 the king raised his standard at Nottingham in a formal declaration that hostilities had begun.

1 The Views of Historians

This volume is concerned with events up to the opening of the Long Parliament in November 1640. What happened after that will be discussed in another book in this series. However, it is impossible completely to ignore the civil war that broke out in 1642, which is justifiably regarded as one of the most crucial episodes in English history. Most of the books on the subject look at the years 1603-40 in the light of what was to come. This colours the accounts which are given of the early seventeenth century because most historians regard the civil war either as a conflict which became inevitable soon after James I became king, or as an accident which could easily have been avoided. The first view, which sees one event leading inexorably to the next - a progressive interpretation - has been held by Whig and Marxist historians. The account which puts more emphasis on short-term causes has been given by revisionists. To understand the thinking behind most books on the early seventeenth century it is necessary to look briefly at the main schools of thought on the civil war.

The Whig and Marxist schools both see the civil war as a major turning point in British history. The Whig tradition which was dominant in the nineteenth and early twentieth centuries saw the civil war as part of a long-term process to establish enlightened parliamentary democracy and religious freedom. In this version parliament was the defender of law, property rights and individual liberties against the attacks of an autocratic monarchy. In increasingly bitter divisions over religion and constitutional issues, parliament acted in a conscious way to promote the interests of the subject. This analysis is now seen as over-simple, the product of a greater confidence about Britain's place in the world and the superiority of the British system of government at a time when the British Empire covered half of the globe and was considered to be a great civilising force. Its greatest exponent, S.R. Gardiner, is now consulted for his painstaking work on the detail of the period rather than for his conclusions.

In the mid-twentieth century a new interpretation was put forward. This was the Marxist view. This argued that at the root of the civil war were social and economic changes which created political divisions. The civil war was the 'bourgeois revolution' of Marxist theory which opened the way to capitalism and the eventual revolution which would overthrow the state. This interpretation came under fierce attack in the mid-1960s partly because a series of local studies proved that neat national classifications could not be used without considerable caution. This has not entirely silenced the Marxist voice. Christopher Hill is its most distinguished proponent and he continues to stress that the mid-seventeenth century was a crucial turning point not only in economic and social developments but also in politics and culture. In the 1970s a new school of thought emerged, that of revisionism. Many historians took up the revisionist stance but the most influential has been Conrad Russell whose work is required reading for those who are interested in the early seventeenth century. The revisionists have sought to get away from the idea that the civil war was inevitable, which was a central tenet of both the Whig and the Marxist interpretations. They have stressed the short-term, almost accidental, nature of the war and especially the short-sighted and obstinate behaviour of Charles I. The monarchy has been seen as the innovator attacking personal liberties and religious orthodoxy. It has been argued that parliament, far from seeking to bring about reform, was merely trying to maintain its ancient privileges and to preserve its view of the relationship between the king and itself. The revisionists have argued that there were structural weaknesses in the machinery of government, especially the crown's inadequate financial resources, but they have denied that there were major divisions over political principle even if the actions of Charles I did provoke considerable resistance. This view sees the political nation as fundamentally united about the nature and purposes of government, but divided over the best way to restore the harmony that everyone wanted.

Revisionists have also made use of local studies to argue that there was a divergence between national and local concerns which produced conflict. MPs were all members of local communities and would often put the interests of their neighbours above that of the crown. The role of Arminianism, the ceremonial anti-Calvinist brand of churchmanship which Charles favoured but which looked to many contemporaries as a first step to Catholicism, has also been given considerable prominence. It has been seen as the single most important factor in destroying the broad consensus which had existed in religion in that it awakened alarm about Charles's ultimate intentions which could give many of his actions a sinister aspect in an age which identified Catholicism with absolutism.

The post-revisionists have looked critically at the revisionist position and have modified some aspects of it. In particular they have argued that important issues of principle did divide the political nation, especially on the nature of royal power and over theories of resistance to unjust rule. The post-revisionists believe it is important to set the civil war in its British context. Too often, they have argued, it is seen merely as the English civil war when events in Scotland and Ireland - both of which rebelled against their king first - were crucial to what happened in England. Among the more accessible post-revisionist writers are Richard Cust and Ann Hughes.

With these broad categories in mind, you should be able to identify the underlying beliefs of the books that you study. If clashes between the king and parliament are portrayed as a battle in which the House of Commons gradually realised its strength, then you will be reading a Whig interpretation. If, on the other hand, the author seeks to show that no conflict was intended and it was all a result of misunderstanding, that will be a revisionist account. If you keep these differences in mind it will help you to synthesize (join together) accounts which seem to tell a different story to produce your own analysis of the course of events.

2 Studying the Topic

Despite the tendency of historians to focus on the civil war that was to come, the early seventeenth century is full of interest in its own right. To understand what contemporaries were thinking and feeling at the time, unaware of impending catastrophe, you must forget what was to follow. The most important domestic issue was the deterioration in the relations between the crown and parliament and why this should have happened. You will find one account given in this volume, but it would be totally acceptable for you to develop an alternative interpretation. As you read through the book ask yourself the following questions at each point of conflict. Why was this problem not settled without ill-feeling? What did each side hope to achieve? Did they do so? If not, what was the reason for failure? What did each side believe about the intentions of the other? Could there have been a solution if people had acted differently or were there underlying problems that were very difficult to solve? In this way you should gradually develop your own ideas about the state of relations between the king and parliament and whether it was likely to lead to more serious trouble in the future.

The second major theme which linked in to both domestic and foreign affairs was religion. The Church of England underwent a dramatic change in the reign of Charles I, as he sought to introduce highly ceremonial worship which reminded many of Catholicism. There are five key questions in this area. Was there real religious harmony in James I's reign? What was the state of the Church in the early seventeenth century? Was there justification for introducing Arminian reforms? Would Arminianism have been perceived as a serious threat if there had not been open Catholic worship at court under Charles I? What was the role of the Puritans who wanted a church free from all taint of popery?

The final two sets of issues concern first, England's place in Europe, especially as the premier Protestant power and second, the direction of Charles I's government. Did England have a moral duty to aid her struggling fellow Protestants in Germany? Did Charles intend to set up an absolute state on the French model? Was the neutrality of the 1630s, with its pro-Spanish bias, part of a plot to undermine the religion of the country? Was the attempt to impose the new prayer book on Scotland part of the same design? The answers to some of these questions may seem obvious but why were they asked at the time, and what effect did this sort of questioning have on politics? Often it is not reality but what men believe to be happening that has the greatest influence on events.

In order to simplify the subject somewhat this book has been divided into three chronological chapters (3, 5 and 7) and two subject chapters, on foreign affairs (4) and religion (6). The latter cover the entire period and obviously have a bearing on events in the chronological chapters. Although cross references are made in the text, it would be wise when reading the chronological chapters to keep asking yourself what are the religious/foreign policy implications of particular events? Equally, when reading the subject chapters ask what effect each situation would have had on domestic affairs. One point that needs emphasis is the central role of religion. Many of the details of theological difference may now seem rather obscure and petty, but in the seventeenth century people were prepared to die and to kill for their religion (or denomination as we would say now). Religion stirred the deepest passions and this should be remembered particularly about the period from 1618 when the Thirty Years War broke out and also about the reign of Charles I with his apparent leanings towards Catholicism.

CHAPTER 2

Britain in 1603

What kind of country did James inherit in 1603? He himself had high expectations of his new territories: he described himself as being 'like a poor man wandering about 40 years in a wilderness and barren soil, and now arrived at the land of promise'. Certainly becoming King of England represented a big step up for the sovereign of Scotland. Not only was England and the countries that went with her - Ireland and Wales - larger and richer, but also the ruler of England was a force to be reckoned with on the European stage and could make a plausible claim to being the leader of the European Protestants. By contrast, Scotland was relatively poor, weak and backward. The nobility and church (or kirk) wielded much of the effective power and there was a much greater sense of being on the margins of European culture especially as the strict Presbyterianism (a system of church government without bishops which gave considerable responsibility to individual congregations) had brought a rift in the 'Auld Alliance' between France and Scotland.

1 English Society

England was not, perhaps, quite as rich as James would have liked to believe. The population approximately doubled between 1500 and 1650 but agricultural production was not able to increase at the same rate. Pressure on resources led to inflation and there was insufficient industry to soak up the increase in manpower, thus creating unemployment. This led to the appearance in England for the first time of a large sub-class which had no land and which existed on the margins of society scraping a living from whatever occasional work could be found. In times of harvest failure this group was especially vulnerable and in the bad times of the 1620s there were actual deaths from famine, something which had not been seen in England for centuries. This background of increased pressure on resources should be borne in mind when looking at the tax demands made by the early Stuart kings.

At the same time as the poor were getting poorer, the rich were getting richer. The increased population meant that landlords could charge higher rents and entry fines to take up a lease. For example, the rents of the manor at Stoneleigh in Warwickshire increased from £418 in 1599 to £1,440 in 1640. Landowners could also benefit from the higher market price their products would command. With income being redistributed from the poor to the rich and with no police force or army to enforce order, what kept society from falling apart?

At one level the answer lies in the acceptance of authority by the common people. Government directives were enforced by Justices of the Peace (JPs) who were chosen from the ranks of the nobility and gentry. There were certain expectations, for example that food would be provided at a reasonable cost in times of scarcity, and if these expectations were not met a riot might break out. Rioting was the means by which common people drew attention to a grievance. It was their only means of attracting attention and it was usually very orderly. Violence against people was rare and a specific target was the focus of attack such as a tithe barn in times of scarcity, or enclosure fences when unemployment was high. The authorities recognised that rioters were not rebels and they were seldom severely punished - fining or whipping were the most common sanctions - but more importantly, action was usually taken to satisfy the legitimate grievances of the rioters.

Society was seen as a single unit with inter-dependent parts and this encouraged a sense of order and authority. For example, the country was like a body with the king as the head, or the commonwealth was described as a tree. There was a 'great chain of being' stretching from God to the lowest forms of life and beyond in which each creature had its appointed place. This was transferred to the social sphere to give divine sanction to the high degree of social stratification and inequality which characterised English society. As Mrs C.F. Alexander put it 200 years later in a famous hymn:

> The rich man in his castle
> The poor man at his gate
> God made them high and lowly
> He ordered their estate.

Just as each person's place in society was divinely ordained, so each person had duties which it was their responsibility to God and their neighbour to discharge. Thus the nobility and gentry could expect service from their tenants but they were expected in return to provide protection, employment and sometimes advancement. The upper classes in their turn were in a position of dependence upon the monarch so that the whole of society was linked in a series of relationships and the role of the king was compared to that of the father in a family. As a contemporary put it:

> As the father over one family, so the King as father over many families, extends his care to preserve, feed, clothe, instruct and defend the whole commonwealth.

In this ideal view of society the most dangerous person was the 'masterless man', one who was not bound into the system of allegiance and service. For this reason vagrants, or those with no settled home, were regarded with great suspicion and were often savagely punished, to modern eyes for no crime other than their poverty. But in the seventeenth century the existence of such people seemed to strike at the very foundations of order and to threaten the social structure.

However, it must not be forgotten that the 'great chain of being' was only an ideal rather than an accurate description of reality. Society was not, in fact, static - it was possible to move up or down and men did not always honour their obligations. This had always been the case, but the early seventeenth century saw increasing tension between the ideal and reality with the pressures brought by population growth and inflation. This was a gradual process. There was no sudden deterioration in 1600, rather the accumulated effects of a century of change could no longer be easily absorbed. Enclosure and other changes in agricultural techniques led to fewer people working on the land. Some people lost their traditional places in society and others became unexpectedly successful through exploiting the opportunities open to them. These developments strained the old deferential idea of society and prompted people to think more of their own interests as individuals. There was no breakdown in order but there was an implicit challenge to the traditional fixed view of social organisation which increased feelings of uncertainty especially in those areas most affected by enclosure or the growth of new industries.

2 The Political System

a) The King

The king was the undisputed head of the political system. He determined policy and controlled the distribution of offices (government posts) and gifts. By long custom there were things which the king could do acting on his own authority which were known as the royal prerogative, while other matters required the consent of parliament or of the judges. The royal prerogative included control of foreign policy, war and peace, the regulation of overseas trade and of the coinage and the pardoning of criminals. Since the establishment of a Protestant Church of England, the sovereign had been head of the church and had the power to radically alter religious practice if he so chose. The king also had an overriding duty to preserve the state and was entitled to take such action as he saw fit to do so. The highest form of law was that which was enforceable in the common law courts. This required a statute. The king could issue proclamations which were intended to remedy defects in statutes but only the king-in-parliament (when the king used parliament to achieve his objectives) could pass statute law.

The theoretical powers of the king did not create much dispute but when it came to applying them there were often grey areas when crown and parliament could each make a reasonable case for their own viewpoint. In these circumstances conflicting theories developed to justify each position. The divine right of kings was the name given to the theory which promoted the king's power while those who wished to limit royal actions put their faith in 'the ancient constitution'. The divine right of kings was the principle that monarchs derived their power from God and were accountable only to Him. This meant that representative institutions, such as parliament, existed only at the king's pleasure and that because the king alone possessed political power, he alone was the law maker. There was no safeguard against a tyrannical ruler, only the belief that God would punish him. By contrast, those who believed in the ancient constitution put reliance on the force of tradition. They argued that the common law had been established over the centuries and it therefore could not be denied by one man even if he was the king. The believers in the ancient constitution accepted that the king had prerogatives but they asserted that these could not be used to undermine the liberty of the subject.

In James's reign there was a great deal of talk about the king's prerogative and the privileges of parliament. James adopted an extreme position in his speeches but he was conciliatory in practice and backed away from conflict. He never attempted to impose the prerogative in the way that he appeared to threaten in his speeches. Charles did not share his father's fondness for the sound of his own voice, but his actions were far more extreme. He expected to be obeyed without question and when anyone ventured to oppose the exercise of his authority he was extremely displeased. He believed in the divine right of kings and that he was always in the right. He thought that those who advocated different policies were either misguided or malicious. It was a dangerous doctrine to hold when the system of government was experiencing stress.

b) The Court

The court was the centre of power and the hub of the political system. The court was not a specific place, it revolved around the king and the great officers of state who attended him. The king was expected to listen to the advice of his privy councillors although he was not bound to act upon it. Many of Charles's problems stemmed from the fact that he often ignored his council. In an age of personal rule access to the king was all important: if one had the king's ear things would get done. This is where the Bedchamber became important. The Privy Council was the formal organ of advice and administration but it was sometimes by-passed. The Bedchamber consisted of those personal attendants whom the king appointed to wait upon him. The court was divided into the public outer chambers and the privy lodgings where the king enjoyed some privacy and to which access was strictly controlled. The gentlemen of the chamber passed freely into this inner world and accompanied the king on his trips out of London. This meant that they saw considerably more of the monarch than ordinary courtiers. It has been estimated that James spent approximately half his reign out of London either hunting or on progress. The gentlemen of the chamber had no formal role in the government but their proximity to the king meant that inevitably he was aware of their concerns and needs, and those of their clients.

An example of this was Lord Hay who was showered with gifts, pensions and land by James, good fortune which was entirely owing to his position in the bedchamber. James created resentment because appointments to his Bedchamber were for a long time given to Scotsmen. The first appointment of an Englishman was Buckingham in 1615. A foreign king thus surrounded himself with his unpopular fellow-countrymen and the English, who continued to hold all the major offices of state, felt that they were being excluded from the inner circle of power and, equally importantly, that the Scots were receiving a disproportionate amount of royal patronage. In fact James was careful to maintain a balance, because, while the Scots were given the lion's share of gifts and pensions, the English received the vast majority of offices. It was unfortunate that the monetary rewards given to the Scots were more apparent, especially in a time of financial stringency.

It was at court that the major issues were debated and holders of opposing views would seek to win the king's support. For example, in James's reign the Howard group or faction supported friendship with Catholic Spain while an opposing faction including the Archbishop of Canterbury and the Earl of Southampton favoured a more Protestant foreign policy. In these struggles each side would seek to mobilise their strength and use their connections. Factions were composed of those who shared common interests but these might change over time. More reliable allies would usually be found among the ranks of one's relations. Marriage was an important tool that was used to create a network of connections with powerful families, it could also be used to neutralise an opponent or seal a friendship. Buckingham used his numerous relatives to build up alliances with many of the major families in the country.

The existence of factions was closely linked to the workings of the patronage system. A young man who was anxious to succeed in political circles would acquire a patron whom he would support and serve in whatever way was required. He might also make gifts to his patron and in return the patron would advance his client's interests and seek to secure a favourable position for him. It was a mark of political power to have a large number of clients. This was a two way process: being in a position of power would attract men who were eager for office or favours, but also having a large number of political adherents, provided their loyalty could be maintained, gave a man considerable power and influence because it would be in the government's interest to have that power base on its side. The patronage system was never static. It was necessary for an ambitious noble always to strive to improve his position. In the 1620s, the Duke of Buckingham monopolised the lion's share of the available patronage and was overwhelmed with requests for help from would-be clients, yet even he believed it was worth his while to win over the Earl of Pembroke, head of an opposing faction, by arranging a marriage alliance between the two families.

In Charles's reign the system of patronage and faction which provided the king with a range of views and prevented any one group from becoming too powerful was not allowed to operate effectively. Charles preferred to rely first on the Duke of Buckingham and then on a small group of advisers. In these circumstances those who wished the country to follow a different course turned to parliament and involved the Commons in what hitherto would have been a court battle. It was a serious mistake of Charles not to contain such disputes within the court and one for which he paid a heavy price.

c) Parliament

Notions of deference pervaded the political sphere. In parliament members were always extremely polite when they addressed or talked about the king. This initially misled James I into confusing deference with subservience. He was used to the plain speaking of the Scottish parliament where members spoke their minds but whose power was limited. The English parliament might be polite but it knew its rights and would not let any challenge to its liberties pass unnoticed. James I had conflicts with his parliaments from the start when there was trouble over a disputed election in Buckinghamshire (see pages 33-4). It is therefore easy to see the king and parliament as opponents, each seeking to undermine the other and win a tactical advantage. Nothing could be further from the truth. The traditional view was that the king was at his most powerful when parliament was in session because the king-in-parliament could enact statute laws (instead of mere proclamations) and obtain additional taxes (or subsidies) from his subjects. Both James and the members of his parliaments agreed with this view and even Charles I would have acknowledged that he could achieve more with parliament, provided that parliament would do as he wished. In the middle ages the tradition was established that criticism could be expressed in parliament but there was no question of undermining the authority of the monarch. The right to freedom of speech was intended to provide the sovereign with good advice unhindered by fear of reprisals.

The king ruled, the privy council advised him and parliament presented the grievances of the people and, if invited to do so, might also offer counsel. If the king chose to ignore their advice as he had the right to do, parliament could register a protest by refusing to grant any subsidies that might be requested. Increasingly in the early seventeenth century, this was a course MPs chose to take. The long years of war (1588-1604) at the end of Elizabeth's reign and the consequent heavy financial demands made upon the country through parliament had produced the conditions in which crown decisions were questioned. Members expected their views to be considered by the monarch if there were to be frequent requests for money.

The king's ordinary revenue was intended to be sufficient for his usual needs with parliament granting extraordinary taxation in times of emergency. As inflation reduced the crown's real income this control over extraordinary supply gave parliament a valuable bargaining point which began to affect the balance of power between it and the king. Harmony remained the ideal to which everyone paid lip service but as it became increasingly difficult to reconcile the wishes of both sides, parliament was ready to exploit its new position.

Parliament was the meeting place of the king and his representatives in the localities. Here policies could be explained and approval sought, serious disquiet could be expressed and policies could be modified. Parliament was a national institution but it spent much of its time dealing with local grievances. When enough of these grievances coalesced, the sovereign and his advisers would take note, if they were wise, and seek to deal with the problem. National and local concerns overlapped. The MPs who passed laws and voted for subsidies were often the same men who would have the responsibility of enforcing or collecting them, as many MPs also acted as Justices of the Peace.

Parliaments were an important part of government but they were irregular and the timing and length of sessions was entirely at the king's discretion. Members did not expect to be summoned for more than a few months at a time; the ideal was to hear the king's needs, respond in an appropriate way with counsel and financial supply if necessary, express the concerns of their constituencies and then return to their localities. Some parliaments passed no legislation and most laws were about relatively minor matters. The two main functions of parliament were expressed by Lord Chancellor Bacon in 1621: 'the one for the supplying of your estates; the other for the better knitting of the hearts of your subjects unto your Majesty'. In an age which did not have newspapers, the propaganda importance of parliament should not be under-estimated. It was a useful forum for informing the country about the direction of royal policy and explaining unpopular policies.

Parliament was made up of the House of Lords and the House of Commons. Members of the Commons were elected by 40 shilling freeholders (those who owned land worth at least 40 shillings a year) in the counties and by a more varied franchise in towns. The majority of elections were not contested, although some produced fierce contests. Most MPs came from the ranks of the wealthy landed gentry and they would often agree amongst themselves who should stand for parliament. This meant that the electorate had merely to confirm the candidate who had come forward. The Commons were responsible for voting subsidies but in other respects they were far less important than they are today and the lead role was often taken by the House of Lords. The Lords were made up of peers of the realm and also bishops. Most of the king's advisers would be represented in parliament and would take the lead in explaining the crown's position and outlining its needs.

Parliament was not part of the government. There was no equivalent of the modern prime minister and cabinet, their functions were exercised by the king and his ministers. Nor were there any parties in the House of Commons, not even in the sense of a king's party and an opposition. MPs might oppose some strands of government policy but they were likely to agree with other aspects of policy and few MPs maintained a consistent role in opposition. As a result, groupings in the Commons were fluid as members combined on some issues and then diverged. Some MPs sought to use their opposition to force the king to take notice of them and bring them into government. Sir Thomas Wentworth, who became one of Charles I's chief ministers, had been an outspoken parliamentary critic in the 1620s. Even John Pym, leader of the Long Parliament, had initially restrained his attacks on Charles's policies in 1640-1 because he was hoping (in vain) for government office.

3 Ireland

When James became King of England he also became King of Ireland, which for centuries had been ruled with varying success by the alien English. Ireland was not technically an independent kingdom as Scotland was but was more like a colony. The Dublin administration was headed by a Lord Lieutenant or Lord Deputy, the Irish parliament had to implement the laws made in England and the English Privy Council was fully entitled to discuss Irish affairs. A Protestant Church of Ireland had been established on a similar basis to the Church of England. This was imposed on the country and the vast majority of the inhabitants remained Roman Catholics. English politicians tended to ignore that Ireland was a foreign country with its own language (Gaelic) and culture.

There were three different groups in Ireland. The 'mere' or native Irish, who were Catholic, were excluded from taking part in political life with a few exceptions. The 'Old English' were the descendants of pre-Reformation English settlers. They were often Catholic and as owners of one third of the profitable land in Ireland they were accustomed to think of themselves as the island's natural rulers. They felt increasingly threatened by the third group, the 'New English'. These were Protestants who had arrived since the Reformation and who controlled the government in Dublin. In general they favoured a policy of plantation to introduce more Protestant settlers often at the expense of the 'mere' Irish. Ireland was usually a drain on the English exchequer and English authority was precarious enough to require an army to maintain it. In the 1590s there had been an uprising in Ulster led by the Earl of Tyrone which finally collapsed in 1603, but his position was not destroyed. An uneasy truce developed which could not be sustained for long.

4 Scotland

'The air might be wholesome but for the stinking people that inhabit it' was a typical English comment on the Scots whom they regarded with fear and loathing. One of James's most cherished projects was a union between England and Scotland, but the English were unwilling to concede a single extra privilege to the Scots just because they shared the same ruler. So Scotland remained an independent state with its own parliament, religion, legal system and local government. In comparison to England, Scottish government was under-developed. There were weaker links between the centre and the localities and there was less taxation because the government played a smaller part in people's lives. The king was entitled to sit and vote in parliament which had a long tradition of advising and criticising the king. The Scottish Church was Presbyterian and Calvinist - there were no bishops and each congregation elected its own elders. The General Assembly provided a meeting place where decisions about religious matters could be taken at a national level. James took great care to ensure that the General Assembly did not take decisions which would be detrimental to him by appearing in person at the Assembly and carefully managing debates.

James had become King of Scotland when he was still a baby after the abdication and flight to England of his mother, Mary Queen of Scots. His mother had also become monarch while she was a child and for 40 years after the death of James V in 1642 there was no effective royal government in Scotland, apart from Mary's six year rule which ended disastrously for her. This had enabled the nobility to seize a disproportionate share of power and had also provided the opportunity for Church leaders under John Knox to oppose royal wishes and establish a radical Protestant church. James spent much of his adult life undermining the position of the nobility and manipulating factions to his advantage. By the time he left Scotland he had redressed the balance of power and successfully subdued the nobility. He recognised the strength of the Church and had been careful not to alienate it. From 1603 Scotland had to endure an absentee monarch with all that implied for reduced favour and positions and unremedied grievances. It is a tribute to James's reign as James VI that Scotland was to cause no trouble in his lifetime. Unfortunately his son did not display the same tact and sensitivity and, in 1638, Scotland was the first of the three kingdoms to rebel.

5 Implications of the Accession of James I

The end of one dynasty and the establishment of a new one was bound to cause some problems. The new king would need to create a sense of loyalty, probably by some well-judged generosity. The ease with which James VI of Scotland became James I of England surprised many onlookers. In large part this was because James had developed close links with Elizabeth's chief minister, Robert Cecil, created Earl of Salisbury by James. It was in both their interests for James's accession to be as trouble-free as possible and there was no hesitation in proclaiming James as the new king. He assumed the role as soon as the news reached him of Elizabeth's death.

The nation heaved a collective sigh of relief at having an active male on the throne again after half a century of being ruled by women. The myth of the golden age of Elizabeth did not begin to appear for another twenty years when disillusionment with Stuart rule was setting in. James was welcomed by his new subjects but there were reservations. What would be the position of his Scottish followers? Would James respect the English political system? What policy would he follow in religion? One might say there was a mood of enthusiastic trepidation as people waited to see what James would do.

a) Politics

In the sixteenth and seventeenth centuries official salaries were so low as to be almost meaningless and courtiers and office holders relied upon the crown to make grants of many different kinds. There were monopolies (the exclusive right to sell a commodity); the right to collect crown debts; grants of customs; the right to issue licences, for example to alehouses; rights of wardship (administering the estate of a minor) and many others. These were all forms of patronage along with the more obvious titles, pensions and grants of land, with which the sovereign could buy support, reward a favourite or keep a potentially discontented faction happy.

Elizabeth I had been very tight-fisted. She was anxious not to run into deficit on her ordinary account and she watched her expenditure like a hawk. This meant that she gave away very little in the way of pensions, offices, titles or gifts especially in the last years of the reign. By the time of James I's accession there was enormous pent up demand from unsatisfied courtiers. It would have been almost impossible for any king to withstand the pressure to be more generous and James was an alien king who had to ensure loyalty among his new subjects as well as desiring to reward his faithful followers. It was, therefore, inevitable that he would dispense more patronage than Elizabeth had. Unfortunately James was generous to a fault. He was incapable of saying no to any request from a favourite and he loved to shower rewards on those around him. He pointed out in 1610 that 'a king's liberality must never be dried up altogether, for then he can never maintain nor oblige his servants and well deserving subjects'. But James's liberality knew no bounds. In one famous incident on his journey south he created 46 knights before breakfast! This excessive lavishness was counter-productive because it devalued the gift and encouraged further demands, impoverishing the crown to little effect.

Parliament was to have much to say about patronage.

b) Finance

The scale of James's giving had serious implications for finance, as did his general extravagance. Elizabeth had been very careful to restrain her expenditure so that she would not be dependent upon parliament for her ordinary revenue. At her death she had left a surplus of £90,000 in the treasury and the debt of £400,000 was covered by outstanding debts owed by France and the Dutch and by an uncollected subsidy voted in 1603. This was an impressive achievement given that England had been at war with Spain for fifteen years and there had been a major rebellion in Ireland in the 1590s. It contrasted very sharply with James's financial position within three years of coming to the throne. Despite making peace he had already accumulated a debt of £816,000 by 1606 through unbridled extravagance and generosity. This extravagance was obvious to everyone. He had been king for less than a year when the Archbishop of York warned him that 'he would exhaust the treasure of the kingdom and bring many inconveniences' and James himself acknowledged in 1610 that he had been too lax with money when he promised that 'the vastness of my expenditure is past which I used in the first two or three years after my coming hither'.

It has been customary to put all the blame for the crown's financial troubles in his reign on to James himself. Recently, an alternative view has been put forward, especially by Conrad Russell, that the financial and administrative machinery of government could not cope with the increased demands placed upon them by inflation and the cost of an active foreign policy. A radical overhaul of the system was needed but this could not be achieved without enormous political upheaval, and in the event it took a civil war to manage it. In the meantime great tensions were created by the act of trying to make the old system work. In this analysis Elizabeth appears in a less favourable light. Although she managed her own finances remarkably successfully, she often did so at the cost of her successors. We have already seen that she deferred the legitimate expectations of her courtiers for rewards which James would be under great pressure to satisfy. Another effect of the policy had been that officials had turned to other means of compensating themselves by bribery or extortion and this had created an atmosphere of corruption. Other economies like cutting the consumption of the royal household were short term and unpopular. More seriously the queen had not attempted to increase royal revenue so it kept pace with inflation which was the only long-term solution to the problem of finance. Elizabeth's policy had been to cut expenditure and if all else failed to sell crown lands which impoverished the crown in the future. This meant that in Elizabeth's reign there was no increase in customs duties as laid down in the Book of Rates and there was no attempt to exploit the crown lands effectively. In 1587 a 50 year lease on some crown property in Bermondsey was agreed at a rent of £68 a year. In 1636 when the lease fell in, it was found to be worth £1,071 a year.

There was scope for improvement in royal revenue but it could only be achieved at a political cost and if Elizabeth had tackled the problem there would have been less ground to make up. The Stuarts were also hit by a fall in the value of the parliamentary subsidy because the local elites responsible for land valuations on which the subsidy was based tended grossly to under-assess themselves and their neighbours. Thus the yield of each subsidy fell from about £130,000 in the mid-sixteenth century to £55,000 by 1628, and this at a time of inflation. So the real value had gone down even more. The Commons failed to appreciate this fully and were reluctant to vote additional sums to make up the deficit. MPs could not understand why the crown made such poor use of their generosity.

c) Religion

Under Elizabeth the Church of England had become firmly established in the country. Few people retained a memory of the Catholicism under Mary and the number of practising Catholics was dwindling. Everyone had to attend their parish church each Sunday, by law, or face a fine for recusancy. This had implanted in most people a strong belief in the correctness of the Protestant creed and the error of the Catholic faith. It was a commonly held idea in the early modern age that religious dissent equalled political dissent and that for a country to harbour members of another creed was to invite political subversion or rebellion. This had proved itself true often enough to give real substance to the belief. In England the plots surrounding Mary, Queen of Scots and the plans to assassinate Elizabeth had made all Catholics seem potential traitors and war with Spain had brought the prospect of Catholic domination once more.

In fact, most English Catholics were peaceful and law abiding but they wanted an opportunity to worship in private unmolested and an end to the recusancy fines, which, if strictly enforced, could ruin a family. In 1603 Thomas Tresham who had paid out more than £2000 in recusancy fines presented a petition for more lenient treatment of Catholics. It was known that James was a tolerant man who liked to follow a middle way and the Catholics hoped that in the new reign they would be freed from the fear of practising their faith.

At the opposite end of the religious spectrum were the Puritans. These were people who wished to 'purify' the Church of the last vestiges of Catholic worship. These included an end to the ring in marriage, signing with the cross at baptism, bowing at the name of Jesus or wearing vestments (clergymen's robes). These were seen as relics of a superstitious past which could lead the unwary into error. Puritans put far greater stress on the preaching of the word by which they meant explaining the Bible, and the individual's response to the message of God. They attached far less importance to the power of the sacraments (baptism and communion) or to the role of worship. In the 1580s there had been an upsurge in Puritanism with some people advocating a Presbyterian system which would have swept away the bishops. This had been suppressed by Elizabeth and the Archbishop of Canterbury and by the end of the reign there was little trouble from the Puritans. However, their hopes of reform had merely been deferred and the arrival of a king from Presbyterian Scotland inevitably created new expectations. On James's way south he was presented with the millenary petition, so called because it was supposedly signed by 1000 clergy. This made a number of moderate requests such as not using the sign of the cross in baptism and prompted James to hold a conference at Hampton Court to discuss the issues (see page 90). This failed to produce the desired reforms and helped create a background of discontent which was to come to the fore under Charles I.

d) Foreign Policy

As King of Scotland, James VI had been on the periphery of European affairs. Scotland was a relatively insignificant nation and the actions of her king were not regarded with much interest by other European states, except France which valued their alliance against England. It was a very different matter when he became James I. At a stroke he became sovereign of the most powerful Protestant state in Europe and if he so wished, he could assume leadership of the European Protestants.

James inherited a war with Spain and alliance with the Dutch who were fighting to win their independence. His wife was Danish so there were strong connections with Denmark which was an important Protestant power. The German Protestant princes were individually too weak to lead the Protestant world and would welcome a more active role from England. But James had no desire to place himself at the head of a Protestant crusade. He abhorred violence, possibly as a result of the feuding of the nobles in his early life and the tragic life of his mother. War was also repugnant to him and he spent his life trying to avoid being sucked into conflicts. James desired to act as a mediator and peace maker. This would involve being on good terms with all sides but a policy which had worked when he was King of Scotland could not succeed in England whose position was very different. The rest of Europe was unconcerned if Scotland was neutral but it was much harder for England to sit on the sidelines without favouring one side in a conflict at the expense of the other. Such a policy was incomprehensible to his subjects and led to a souring of relations with parliament as the king sought to balance the Protestant marriage of his daughter with a Spanish Catholic match for his son.

The idealism of James's foreign policy is undoubted. The question for the historian is whether such a policy was possible in a Europe torn apart by religious rivalries. Could James as ruler of England hope to maintain neutrality and act even-handedly between the two parties to the Thirty Years War or did his position force him to take sides so that his unwillingness to do so harmed the monarchy and the country?

One further point should be considered. An active foreign policy was extremely expensive, especially as military costs rose faster than general inflation and could not be financed for long out of ordinary expenditure. A war would place the monarch in a position of much greater dependence upon parliament. The king had sole responsibility for the direction of foreign policy but if parliament disliked it they could refuse to grant taxes to finance it. This was to lead to major problems in the 1620s with repercussions not only for foreign affairs but also for the conduct of domestic policy.

Making notes on 'Britain in 1603'

This is an introductory chapter. It is more important to understand the structure of society in the seventeenth century than it is to write down every example. Look at the flow diagram and make sure you understand how the different parts of the political structure related to each other. If you have a clear picture of how the system worked in theory you will be able to spot when events did not conform to this pattern. Read the first section on English society again and write a paragraph from memory describing how society was organised. Then use the following headings to make brief notes on the function of each part of the political system.

a) The King
b) The Court
    i)   The Privy Council
    ii) The Bedchamber
c) The Patronage System
d) Parliament

Finally, make notes on the potential problems which faced James on his accession using the headings in the chapter. Include in this section the position of Scotland and Ireland and the possible trouble that could arise from having an absent king.

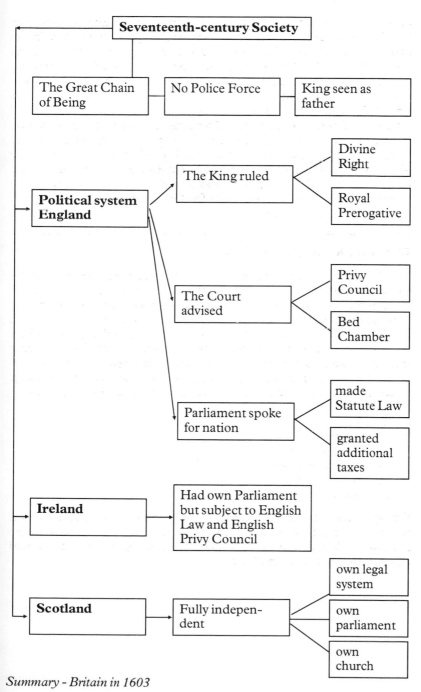

Seventeenth-century Society

The Great Chain of Being — No Police Force — King seen as father

Political system England

The King ruled
- Divine Right
- Royal Prerogative

The Court advised
- Privy Council
- Bed Chamber

Parliament spoke for nation
- made Statute Law
- granted additional taxes

Ireland — Had own Parliament but subject to English Law and English Privy Council

Scotland — Fully independent
- own legal system
- own parliament
- own church

Summary - Britain in 1603

CHAPTER 3

Domestic Politics, 1603-18

The reign of James I can be divided into two: the period before the rise of the Duke of Buckingham, and the time when Buckingham dominated the Court and politics. This division coincides neatly with events in Europe because as Buckingham rose to power so the events which ushered in the Thirty Years War were set in motion. This chapter will cover the first period - the years up to 1618. During this time James established himself as King of England and many of the problems which would prove so difficult to resolve were revealed. These included the king's extravagance, the inadequacy of royal revenue, increasing disharmony between crown and parliament and disapproval of James's preferred lifestyle.

James retained Robert Cecil as chief minister, a position he had held under Elizabeth since the death of his father over ten years before, and later made him Earl of Salisbury. While Salisbury remained in control up to 1610, James's finances were unsteady but there was hope of reform. Salisbury tried to bring in a new system by which the king would give up some of his ancient sources of revenue in return for parliamentary subsidies. Unfortunately this 'Great Contract' (1610) failed through lack of trust on both sides and Salisbury lost influence. Thereafter, James lurched from one financial crisis to another, kept afloat by borrowing from the customs farmers.

The king's financial extravagance undermined his relations with parliament which became soured by mutual suspicion. English MPs disliked the favour shown to Scots followers of James and they were utterly opposed to the king's dream of a closer union with their northern neighbours. James was ready to work with his parliaments but he showed great lack of tact in the way he addressed them, often stating that they were totally dependent upon him and was then irritated when they responded with affronted dignity and restated their privileges. There was a genuine desire on both sides to work together, but often it failed to be translated into political harmony and acrimonious debates were a feature of parliamentary sessions.

These years saw the appearance of the Jacobean court which was very different from both its predecessor and its successor. Contemporaries were shocked by its lack of formality, the bawdy talk, the excessive feasting when many participants would end up under the table and by the way James would fondle and intimately address the handsome young men of his entourage. This gave rise at the time to unfavourable comment and has contributed to the bad press which James has received from historians.

1 The Character of James I

What kind of a man was James? The answers have been extraordinarily diverse. Some of the more extreme descriptions make him seem little better than a wild animal, and yet the opinion of contemporaries who observed him as King of Scotland were far more complimentary. These accounts give contrasting views. The first was written by M. de Fontenay, envoy from Mary Queen of Scots, to his brother in 1584.

1 [James] is for his age [18] the premier prince who has ever lived. He has three qualities of the soul in perfection. He apprehends and understands everything. He judges reasonably. He carries much in his memory and for a long time. In his questions he is lively and
5 perceptive, and sound in his answers ... In brief he has a marvellous mind, filled with virtuous grandeur and good opinion of himself.

His manners, as a result of the failure to instruct him properly, are aggressive and very uncivil, both in speaking, eating, clothes, games, and conversation in the company of women. I have noted
10 in him only three defects which may possibly be harmful to the conservation of his estate and government. The first is his ignorance and failure to appreciate his poverty and lack of strength, overrating himself and despising other princes. The second that he loves indiscreetly and obstinately despite the disapprobation of his
15 subjects. The third, that he is too idle and too little concerned with business, too addicted to his pleasure, principally that of the chase.

The second was written by a courtier, Sir Anthony Weldon, after James had died.

1 He was of a middle stature, more corpulent through his clothes than in his body ... his clothes ever being made large and easy, the doublets quilted for stiletto-proof ... He was naturally of a timorous disposition ... his eyes large, ever rolling after any
5 stranger that came in his presence ... His beard was very thin; his tongue too large for his mouth, which made him speak full in the mouth and made him drink very uncomely, as if eating his drink, which came out of the cup at each side of his mouth. His skin was as soft as taffeta sarsnet [a thin silk], which felt so because he
10 never washed his hands, only rubbed his finger ends slightly with the wet end of a napkin; his legs were very weak, having had, (as was thought), some foul play in his youth ... that weakness made him ever leaning on other men's shoulders; his walk was ever circular, his fingers ever in that walk fiddling about his cod piece ...
15 He was very liberal of what he had not in his own grip, and would rather part with £100 he never had in his keeping that one twenty shilling piece within his own custody ... A very wise man was wont

to say that he believed him the wisest fool in Christendom, meaning him wise in small things, but a fool in weighty affairs.

Look carefully at these two accounts. Which seems to be more unbiased and trustworthy? Consider the background of the writers. M. de Fontenay had been sent by James's mother. Sir Anthony Weldon hated the Scots and wrote a most abusive pamphlet about them of which a typical example is: 'To be chained in marriage with one of them (Scots) were to be tied to a dead carcass and cast into a stinking ditch.' James found out about the pamphlet and dismissed Weldon from his court position. Weldon got his revenge by writing his savage attack on James which has coloured uninformed opinion of the king ever since. The judgement of more discerning historians would agree with de Fontenay that James was intelligent, that he had appalling manners, that he often over-estimated his position in foreign affairs, that his fondness for young male favourites was very unpopular and that he neglected state matters to indulge his passion for hunting.

Many of James's personality traits can be traced back to his childhood. Deprived of both his parents as a baby (his mother was probably an accomplice in the murder of his father) he grew up as a lonely boy who was to crave affection throughout his life. His marriage to Anne of Denmark became loveless after a successful start. James turned to a series of young men, beginning in the 1580s with his cousin Esme Stewart, later Duke of Lennox. These supplied the family life that James had never known as a child and was unable to successfully create as an adult despite having two sons, Henry and Charles, and one daughter, Elizabeth, who survived into adulthood. It is striking that James's relations with Buckingham, his last favourite, were more cordial than with his own son Charles. James signed his letters to Buckingham 'your darling Dad' and addressed him as 'Steeny'. It is uncertain whether James was a practising homosexual but contemporaries were scandalised by the way he caressed his favourites in public and resentful of the honours he heaped upon them. James had no one on whom to model himself as king. It is unfortunate that his manners, which were extremely coarse, had not been corrected as a child. Persuading the king not to lecture his subjects, which he was inclined to do after he became King of England, might have been more difficult. James liked to prove the correctness of his position by lengthy explanations, but the unfortunate members of the English parliament did not enjoy the king haranguing them for hours at a time. James went so far as to apologise for this in 1621 'I never meant to weary myself or you with such tedious discourses as I have done heretofore'.

The positive side of this aspect of James's character was his love of learning. He was genuinely interested in philosophy and theology and he wrote a number of books including *The Trew Law of Free Monarchies* which was a justification of the divine right of kings and *Basilikon Doron*

The family tree of James I. Engraving by Benjamin Wright, 1619

which set out his views on religion. James was unusually tolerant for the early seventeenth century and the execution of Catholic priests virtually ended in his reign.

Another part of James's character that attracted unfavourable contemporary comment was his lack of physical courage. There had been a number of plots against him when he was King of Scotland and within three years of his accession to the English throne those involved in the Gunpowder Plot tried to blow up not only the king but the assembled members of the Lords and Commons. So James had good reason to be wary of assassins especially as the death of Henry IV of France in 1610 confirmed the vulnerability of kings. However, contemporaries did not like their sovereigns to show signs of weakness and Sir Anthony Weldon wrote scathingly about James's padded clothes which were designed to prevent a dagger from reaching his body. Along with his fear of personal violence went a much more praiseworthy desire to avoid war. James hated war and sought throughout his reign to keep England from being sucked into one. Ultimately he failed, but much of the blame lies with Buckingham and Prince Charles who exerted great pressure to persuade the king to agree to war against his better judgement.

2 Problems with Finance

The side to James that was to cause him the greatest political problems was undoubtedly his extravagance. We have seen (page 17) that finance would have been a headache for any monarch but James made the problem far worse than it need have been. He did not appreciate that although England was much richer than Scotland, the mechanisms for tapping that wealth effectively in the crown's interest did not exist. Instead, he marvelled at the wealth displayed by the nobility on his journey south and embarked on a colossal spending spree. Between 1603 and 1612 he spent £185,000 on jewels; pensions given as rewards to courtiers rose by £50,000 to £80,000 a year; expenditure on the household doubled by 1610 and the queen and Prince Henry, James's elder son who died in 1612, had their own lavish households which swallowed up more royal revenue. Elizabeth had spent less than £300,000 a year in peace time. Under James this figure rose immediately to £400,000 and reached a peak of £522,000 in 1614. Contemporaries would have minded less about the scale of James's extravagance if it had not gone so largely on conspicuous consumption or into the pockets of the hated Scottish foreigners. One of the Scots who had accompanied James to London was Lord Hay whose extravagance surpassed even the king's. On one occasion he gave a banquet for the French ambassador which occupied 30 cooks for 12 days. The food alone cost £2,200! With examples such as these and the knowledge that the king had paid Lord Hay's debts, it is scarcely surprising that the Commons believed James should be able to manage on the crown's traditional sources of revenue if he practised a bit more economy.

Salisbury tried to restrain James's extravagance by issuing the Book of Bounty in 1608. This prohibited the crown giving away major items such as lands, customs or impositions (customs duties on specific goods). It was designed to lower the expectations of courtiers but it did not succeed, partly because James gave cash instead. In the last four months of 1610 alone he was persuaded to give away over £36,000. The other reason for failure was that no one could afford to oppose the king's wishes for long if he valued his position. So Salisbury, whose idea it had been to issue the Book of Bounty, found himself suggesting the transfer of Sir Walter Raleigh's manor at Sherborne to Robert Carr, the new favourite, as a way of by-passing the rules. (Sir Walter Raleigh's estates had been forfeited to the crown when he was found guilty of high treason in 1604.) For this he earned the gratitude of both king and favourite which was worth more to Salisbury than the long-term financial viability of the crown. The extravagance of James distorted the customary financial relationship between the monarch and his subjects. It was expected that under normal circumstances the crown would not receive additional help from the country in the form of parliamentary subsidies but would live 'of its own' - in other words on its ordinary revenue.

This ordinary revenue came from a number of sources. At the beginning of James's reign the most important was still the crown lands even though Elizabeth had sold over £800,000 worth of estates. It was difficult for the king to maximise his income from land because extracting economic rents was unpopular and the crown lands were a convenient form of patronage. Leases on favourable terms were a way of rewarding courtiers and officials without direct cost to the exchequer. The crown lands diminished in importance throughout the reigns of James and Charles because, as one financial crisis gave way to another, successive Lord Treasurers saw the sale of land as being the quickest and easiest way to raise money. By 1640, crown lands had ceased to be a significant part of crown revenue.

Customs revenue was the second major source of crown finance. Traditional dues on imports and exports, known as tonnage and poundage were normally voted to the monarch for life by the first parliament of the reign. There was considerable scope for improvement in the revenue from customs as they had not been exploited effectively under Elizabeth and the advent of peace would increase trade and with it the yield from customs. By 1621, customs revenue was bringing nearly three times as much as crown lands. In 1604, direct collection of the customs was abandoned and it was farmed out to a syndicate of merchants. In return for an annual rent the customs farmers were able to collect and keep the customs revenue. This had advantages for both sides. It gave the king a regular income which was in excess of what crown officials had paid to the exchequer from the customs. It also provided an additional source of patronage and created a group closely linked to the crown who would probably be willing to make loans when the king was in financial difficulty. For the farmer, the system brought considerable rewards because the crown never demanded a price for the customs that reflected their true worth. The new efficiency of customs collection meant that in effect a new indirect tax had been created. This caused great uneasiness in parliament which saw its control of taxation being undermined. This fear was dramatically increased after 1606 when a merchant, John Bate, was taken to court for refusing to pay a duty on currants which he said had not been sanctioned by parliament. The judges found for the king because he had the right to regulate trade for the security of the realm. Bate's case opened the way to vastly increasing the scope of the customs. In 1608 new duties known as impositions were levied on 1400 articles with no real pretence that it was in the interest of trade. These brought in an additional £70,000 a year to the exchequer and were capable of considerable expansion. By the end of the 1630s the crown was dependent for half its income on customs and receipts had grown to between £300,000 and £400,000 annually.

The third strand in crown finances was made up of feudal tenures and wardship which were relics from the middle ages and which had largely lost their justification by the seventeenth century, although not their financial usefulness to the crown. Feudal tenures dated from the time when major landowners owed a duty of military service to the king who was entitled to take over their property if they died leaving a minor or a woman as heir. Wardship was the name given to the system whereby an estate was managed after the death of its owner until the heir came of age or, in the case of a woman, was married. It was a useful tool for rewarding courtiers who could enrich themselves at the estate's expense and use the marriage of the heir to further their own purposes. For a family, two or more wardships in rapid succession might bring ruin and there were many calls for an end to the system which brought about £65,000 to the crown in 1610. Purveyance was another medieval relic established at a time when the court moved frequently around the country thus ensuring that the burden of its expense did not fall only on one area. Purveyance was the right of the court to buy provisions at fixed prices which were well below market rates. The court could also requisition carts to carry its purchases. This system was open to gross abuse by corrupt officials who could buy excess provisions and then sell them at a profit. It also fell heavily on a small section of the people since the court no longer spent most of its time travelling around the country as had been the case when purveyance was first introduced. It was worth about £40,000 to the court and parliament was anxious to put an end to it, but there was disagreement about whether to compensate the king for his loss of revenue or whether he should merely give up purveyance because it was acknowledged to be an abuse. In the end nothing was done about purveyance because the Commons were afraid that any system of compensation would produce more abuses and there was no chance of the king relinquishing it without adequate financial provision.

The financial problems encountered by James were not all of his own making. With careful management crown revenues would have been sufficient to cover the every day needs of the state, but any additional expenditure, especially military expenditure where costs rose much faster than other items, could only be covered with difficulty. Even though peace had been made with Spain in 1604, military expenditure did not come to an end. In Ireland between 1603 and 1608 £600,000 was spent on the army. In addition, there was expenditure to maintain English garrisons in the Netherlands. These factors tended to be ignored by parliament which did not understand why the crown made such poor use of the funds it granted. MPs looked back to Elizabeth and what she had achieved and, ignoring both inflation and the falling value of the subsidy, attributed the Stuarts' repeated requests for money to incompetence or extravagance, a view that was at least partly justified by the evidence. The system by which the crown received any revenue was riddled with what we would now describe as corruption as royal officials siphoned off some of the money intended for the king to line their own pockets. Everyone involved sought to enrich themselves at royal expense. A good example of this is the Earl of Salisbury, the loyal servant of both Elizabeth and James who was entitled to some reward for his long and faithful service. No one accused him of corruption but a system that enabled him to cream off sufficient profits to build the magnificent palace at Hatfield had flaws. Two examples will show how he managed it - examples that could be repeated for many courtiers, although not everyone had Salisbury's opportunities. In 1609 as master of the court of wards, Salisbury gained £1,400 from a wardship that brought the crown £370. More spectacularly, in 1610 as Lord Treasurer he negotiated the renewal of his farm of the silk duties on the original terms even though the trade had greatly expanded. Instead of the modest profit of £434 which he had originally enjoyed, he was now gaining £7,000 a year. This unscrupulous robbing of the crown coincided with his efforts to put royal finances on a sounder footing by negotiating the Great Contract with parliament (see page 30) and illustrates the problems that would be encountered by anyone attempting to reform the system. Too many people had a vested interest in the system remaining unreformed. As the principle loser was the crown which could not afford to alienate its office holders, it would require a major upheaval to change matters. Parliamentary supply also suffered from self-interest. Those who were liable to pay the subsidy, which excluded the poor, had to declare what they were worth but these assessments were usually a huge under-estimate. Cranfield (Lord Treasurer 1621-4) estimated his total wealth at £90,000 but was taxed on only £150, while Buckingham, the richest man in the kingdom after the king, was apparently worth a mere

£400! Death caused the subsidy rolls to shrink and new families did not make up the numbers. In part of Suffolk, 66 persons had been assessed in 1557 on land and goods worth £521; by 1628 only 37 persons were assessed on £77. When major landowners refused to take a responsible share of the costs of running the kingdom it is small wonder that the crown found itself in trouble, but the glaring fact of James's extravagance enabled the Commons to ignore the fact that their subsidies were worth less and less. Both king and Commons could view the actions of the other as unreasonable with some justification.

It is important to remember that parliamentary supply was becoming less valuable when considering the king's reactions to parliament. It was not always worth his while to bargain for a grant because he might lose more than he gained. A good example of this was impositions, which brought him the equivalent of a subsidy every year. The Commons disliked impositions but there was no guarantee that they would produce compensatory revenue if they were abolished. So in 1614 James dissolved parliament rather than lose control of impositions.

Parliamentary finance was always uncertain as the record of James's reign illustrates. James's first parliament (1604-10) showed itself to be wary about making grants but it was not unco-operative. The first session gave no supply because a large grant made at the end of Elizabeth's reign was still being collected. The second session met in 1606 in the aftermath of the Gunpowder Plot and made the unusually large and unexpected grant of £400,000. This helped to mislead James into believing that parliament would always pay his debts rather than seeing the subsidy as a token of gratitude for his - and their - safety. The grant was passed with the slimmest of majorities (one vote) and this, rather than the king's optimistic view, gave a more realistic picture of the difficulty which James would henceforth experience when trying to get money from parliament. Between 1606 and 1621, James received only one grant (of under £100,000) and by the 1620s disillusion with the crown's handling of its finances made obtaining adequate parliamentary funds an increasing problem. The uncertainty of supply made pursuit of an active foreign policy difficult because only parliament could grant the sums necessary to maintain an army. A new financial system was needed and an attempt to achieve this was made in the Great Contract of 1610.

3 The Great Contract

Salisbury, Lord Treasurer from 1608, was anxious to put the crown's finances on a firmer footing. He increased customs revenue and administered crown lands more efficiently but his most imaginative scheme was a plan to do away with wardship, purveyance and the feudal tenures in return for parliamentary supply and the discharge of the crown debt. Salisbury proposed in 1610 that if the Commons would make a single grant of £600,000 for the debt and give the crown

£200,000 a year, the king would give up his rights to purveyance, wardship and some other lesser revenues. This plan was not without personal cost to Salisbury because as master of the Court of Wards he stood to lose a significant part of his income and it indicates to what lengths he would go to achieve reform. Months of negotiations with the Commons followed and by the summer recess it has been agreed that an annual subsidy of £200,000 would replace purveyance and wardship but there would be no parliamentary grant towards the debt apart from the single subsidy already granted which amounted to about £100,000. Along with the Great Contract went a separate bill which legalized the impositions already made by James in the aftermath of Bate's case but prohibited any new ones without parliamentary sanction. This was a neat way of preserving everybody's interests: the king did not lose out because he kept his impositions and parliament maintained its control over taxation. All that remained was for both bills to be enacted when parliament reassembled in November 1610. Over the summer, amongst both courtiers and MPs, doubts began to surface about the Contract and when parliament resumed its debates the two sides raised their demands. It rapidly became obvious that the Contract was not going to succeed and with it was lost the bill on impositions. James felt let down and humiliated. He had condescended to bargain with parliament over his divinely-given prerogative and he had been rejected. Salisbury had put him in this position and thereafter he lost influence, although he was not removed from his position as Treasurer before his death in 1612.

What went wrong with the Contract which had seemed such a sensible idea? Why did both sides fear that they would get the worst of the bargain? A large part of the answer must be the mistrust which had developed so that neither side would rely on the good intentions of the other. The Commons could not be certain that the king would not accept their grant and continue to pocket the feudal revenues as well. Many MPs disliked the idea of funding the king's extravagance and feared that the Scots would be the major beneficiaries. As one member put it: 'to what purpose to draw a silver stream into the royal cistern if it shall daily run out thence by private cocks'. It had never been clearly established how the money to compensate the king would be raised and this also created uncertainty about the proposals. For his part the king and some of his advisers were also having second thoughts. The Chancellor of the Exchequer calculated that the prerogative revenues which the king was giving up were together worth about £115,000 a year. This would have given the king a net gain of some £85,000 a year which was unlikely to be increased to take account of inflation. The prerogative revenues on the other hand, could be exploited more efficiently to make them very profitable, as Charles I was to demonstrate in the 1630s. The success of the Contract would also have meant that the bill on impositions would have been passed, preventing the king from expanding his revenue from customs. Since customs was the only part of crown revenue capable of increasing significantly, this might seriously impede the king's freedom of action. The surrender of wardship would remove a useful source of patronage from the monarch. Granting a rich manor to a courtier was an easy and cheap way of paying a political debt and the financial compensation might not equal the loss. Looked at from James's short-term view, it is easy to see why he became reluctant to proceed with the Contract. Viewed from a longer-term perspective, the failure of the Great Contract was unfortunate for both the Stuart dynasty and the country. If it had been passed it might have begun the transformation of England's administrative system. Parliament would have taken more responsibility for financing the government and a more systematic way of extracting financial support from the population would have been devised instead of leaving it to the chances of purveyance or wardship. With parliament responsible for raising revenue, it would have understood the problems of government finance more clearly and much of the conflict between the House of Commons and the crown from 1620 to the civil war might have been avoided. However, the scheme came to nothing and these consequences can only be speculations.

4 Years of Drift, 1612-18

The failure of the Contract left the king's finances in a sorry state. Salisbury had reduced the debt from over £600,000 but only by selling £400,000 worth of crown lands. This expedient could not be repeated too often and the debt mounted steadily until it stood at £900,000 in 1618. When Salisbury died in 1612 he was not replaced and the treasury was put in commission (run by a committee) for two years. James did not want to have a chief minister who would control the government but unfortunately he lacked the application to make up for leaving the offices of treasurer and secretary of state vacant. The years 1612 to 1614 saw the government drifting with no sense of direction.

Money was sought in a number of ways. In 1611 the title of baronet was created and sold at a cost of £1,095. By 1614 this had brought in £90,000, but by then the market was saturated and by 1622 the price had fallen to £220 which increased disillusion with honours and the court. When the parliament of 1614 produced no supply, James demanded a 'benevolence' amounting to £65,000 instead of the subsidy which parliament would supposedly have voted if it had not been dissolved. He was also persuaded to give government sanction to an ill-considered scheme involving the cloth trade. Known as Cockayne's scheme, the project was the idea of William Cockayne, a London merchant and alderman. The country's largest export was unfinished cloth which went to the Netherlands. The trade was handled by the Merchant Adventurers and Cockayne wanted to break into their monopoly. He therefore persuaded the king to prohibit the export of unfinished cloth on the grounds that this would generate employment in the finishing of the cloth and increase customs revenue by increasing the value of the product. In fact the opposite happened. Unlike the Merchant Adventurers, Cockayne and his backers did not have the resources to purchase all the cloth produced and unemployment soared in the clothing districts. The Dutch reacted to the attempted attack on their industry by finding new sources of unfinished cloth. In late 1616 exports through London were a third down on their 1614 level and customs revenue fell accordingly. At this point the Merchant Adventurers were allowed to resume their control of the cloth trade which gradually recovered but never again reached the high point of 1614.

In 1614 James decided he needed another Lord Treasurer. Regrettably the choice fell upon the Earl of Suffolk whose corruption surpassed anything yet seen. In his four years as Treasurer, Suffolk built Audley End which was said to have cost at least £80,000, twice the cost of Hatfield. James said that it was too big for a king but fit for a Lord Treasurer! This showed that the king at least had low expectations of his treasurers' honesty. There was widespread selling of offices and men did not bother to hide the profits they were extracting from their positions. The one successful revenue device was the sale of honours, including £10,000 for an earldom. James gave much of the proceeds away in ill-judged generosity and it cheapened the concept of honour. In 1615 there were 27 earls, by 1628 this had risen to 65. While Suffolk was in control, the Crown's debt nearly doubled from £500,000 to £900,000. At last his actions were too much even for James and he was dismissed in 1618 and convicted of embezzlement. At this point the reputation of James's court and the state of his finances reached their lowest ebb.

5 Relations with Parliament

Despite the general good will which had surrounded James's accession there had been some apprehension about his intentions. His reputation had preceded him as the author of *The Trew Law of Free Monarchies* with its emphasis on the divine right of kings: 'Kings were the authors and makers of the law, and not the laws of the king' and 'the king is above the law, as both the author and giver of strength thereto'. In the early seventeenth century, representative institutions were under threat all over Europe as several monarchs sought to end their effectiveness and the English parliament had no desire to wither away. For this reason MPs were very sensitive to any apparent attack upon their privileges and were liable to see a challenge to their status where none was intended.

The first parliament, which met in March 1604, started badly when there was a dispute over the Buckinghamshire election. A privy councillor, Sir John Fortescue, had been defeated by Sir Francis Goodwin but the Chancery Office had declared his election invalid on the grounds that Goodwin had been outlawed for failure to pay his debts. The Commons claimed that they were traditionally the judges of disputed election returns and they immediately reacted to this threat to their independence. After angry speeches by both the king and MPs, both sides backed down from a confrontation and the matter was resolved when the Commons agreed to a new election and the king accepted the House's right to be the judge of its election returns.

Crown and Commons had avoided a nasty clash but it was not a promising beginning and the atmosphere did not improve when it soon became clear that James wished to push forward a full union between his two kingdoms as speedily as possible. 'I am assured that no honest subject of whatsoever degree within my whole dominions is less glad of this joyful union than I am'. He could hardly have been more wrong. The English cordially detested their northern neighbours and regarded their appearance at Court with deep suspicion and loathing. There was nothing they wanted less than a union and the Commons therefore created as many delays as they could to all of James's requests. When they refused to change the country's name to 'Great Britain', James issued a proclamation in October 1604 to announce that he would take the title of 'King of Great Britain'. Both parties had reason to feel irritated, the king because of the Commons' delays and the Commons because James was using his prerogative to make legal changes that rightly should be parliament's business.

The failure of the Union which James continued to seek up to 1610 was a bitter disappointment to him and caused him to lose faith in the Commons. The Commons became increasingly anxious about the king's absolutist tendencies and feared they were being misrepresented to the king so that he looked more harshly on them. One MP believed the Lords deliberately used the Commons to express their own fears on the Union and commented 'yet they clad angel-like were received into Abraham's bosom while we fried in the furnace of the king's displeasure'. At the end of the 1604 session, the Commons produced a statement of their position. This was 'The Form of Apology and Satisfaction', which they entered into their journal although they did not present it to the king. In this the most revealing phrase indicating their state of mind was 'The prerogatives of princes may easily and do daily grow; the privileges of the subject are for the most part at an everlasting stand'. It was easy for the Commons to believe that the king was bent on increasing his power at the expense of their own.

The second session of the first parliament was due to meet on 5 November 1605. In the event it was adjourned because a plot was discovered to blow up the king and all his parliament at the state opening (see page 88). An atmosphere of patriotic thankfulness pervaded the session when it did resume in January 1606. Doubts about the king's extravagance were overcome in a desire to show him how relieved they were that the Gunpowder Plot had failed and James was given the largest peacetime supply that had been known, over £400,000. The session was a short one and by the time the third session began, in the winter of 1606, the Commons had resumed their suspicious attitude. They spent months discussing the Union but failed to arrive at a satisfactory conclusion.

James was unable to compel parliament to legislate for a full union. However, he could partly get round this by using the judges to interpret the law in his favour as he had done in Bate's case. One important aspect of Union was that citizens of one kingdom would automatically be citizens of the other. If a full union had come about this would have applied to everyone, but in an important test case, in 1608, it was decided that Robert Calvin was a naturalised English subject. Calvin was a Scot, born after James came to the throne in England and was therefore known as a *post-nati*. The case was brought on his behalf to test the legal position. Parliament disliked the way the judges were used to substitute for their inaction but there was little they could do about it since the judges were in no way acting improperly. However, this use of the law courts could be seen as an attack upon the position of parliament and it contributed to the growth of mistrust.

The final session of the first parliament was largely taken up with negotiations over the Great Contract. As we have seen there were a number of reasons for the breakdown in negotiations but underlying all of them was the lack of trust between king and parliament. Neither felt the other could be relied on to keep their side of the unspoken agreement between them that the king would rule in the best interests of the country with the advice of his councillors and giving due weight to the petitions of his people as expressed through their representatives, while parliament would supply his necessities and pass any laws that were required. Instead there was a retreat into dogma as James lectured about his prerogative and the Commons made statements about their rights and privileges. It was unhelpful of the Commons to write in the Apology of 1604 that their privileges had been 'more universally and dangerously impugned than ever (as we suppose) since the beginnings of parliaments' because it was obviously a gross exaggeration. Similarly, it was tactless of James to make a speech of two hours to parliament full of sentiments such as

1 Kings are justly called gods for that they exercise a manner or resemblance of divine power upon earth ... They make and unmake their subjects, they have power of raising and casting down, of life and death, judges over all their subjects in all causes, 5 and yet accountable to none but God only.

In his actions James had been careful not to attack directly the privileges of the Commons but king and parliament were pulling in opposite directions. He had shown great skill in managing his Scottish parliaments but he made some elementary mistakes in dealing with his English subjects. One such mistake was to fail to explain crown policies clearly. In part this stemmed from another mistake which was not to ensure sufficient representation for Privy Councillors in the Commons. Lacking adequate information, MPs were often ready to suspect the crown of sinister intentions and were therefore unco-operative. In return James became frustrated and angry. The events of James's second decade as king were to make the rift wider.

6 Robert Carr

In 1607 Robert Carr, a young French-educated Scot, came to James's attention and rapidly achieved the status of chief favourite. As was his custom, James showered Carr with money, offices and titles so that he ended up as Earl of Somerset. While Salisbury was alive Carr's influence was limited but Salisbury's death left a power vacuum at court which was filled by Carr and the Howard family, one of the most influential noble families in the country. In 1613, after a scandalous divorce case, Carr married Frances Howard, Countess of Essex, the daughter of the Earl of Suffolk. The obvious agreement of the king to the divorce caused the reputation of the court to fall and there was concern about the development of a pro-Spanish foreign policy because the Howards were either Catholic or had only a shallow commitment to the Church of England. Spain was the obvious ally for Catholics because of its unwavering commitment to the faith. It was also the strongest European power of the day and was therefore in a better position to help English Catholics than France which had a child (Louis XIII) as king.

In 1614 it was resolved to call a parliament to raise some money. There was no organised programme for this parliament and the Privy Council was divided about whether it should meet. In the absence of clear leadership from the court, the Commons turned to a discussion on impositions. There seemed no prospect of supply being voted and when one MP demanded that the Scottish members of the Bedchamber should be sent home James dissolved parliament after a session lasting only a few weeks. Because it passed no legislation and made no supply this is known as the Addled Parliament. James expressed his frustration to the Spanish Ambassador.

> The House of Commons is a body without a head ... I am surprised that my ancestors should ever have permitted such an institution to come into existence. I am a stranger and found it here when I arrived, so that I am obliged to put up with what I cannot get rid of.

It was another seven years before James met with a parliament and in the meantime he began actively pursuing a Spanish marriage for Charles, the dowry from which would remove the need for another session of parliament for some time. The failure of the Addled Parliament and the dominant position at court of the Howards alarmed the anti-Spanish faction led by the Earl of Pembroke and the Archbishop of Canterbury. They decided to try to entice James's favour away from Carr by introducing a new young man to court. The choice fell upon George Villiers, the eighth child of a member of the Leicestershire gentry, whose prospects would normally have been very limited. The Archbishop of Canterbury, George Abbot, persuaded the queen to ask for Villiers (hereafter referred to as Buckingham) to become a Gentleman of the Bedchamber. In 1615 James was captivated by him and he seems to have impressed everyone he met. Bishop Goodman described him as 'the handsomest-bodied man of England; his limbs so well-compacted and his conversation so pleasing and of so sweet a disposition'. But the appearance of an additional favourite did not result in the immediate fall of Carr. It took the scandal of the Overbury affair to remove him from court.

Sir Thomas Overbury was a close friend and mentor of Robert Carr but he had opposed his marriage to the Countess of Essex. As a result he was put in the Tower on a concocted charge, but the Countess, eager to have him out of the way, arranged to have him poisoned in 1613. News of the murder was kept secret for two years but when the scandal broke, not only the countess but also her husband were found guilty of the murder, although Carr's involvement is less certain. James commuted their sentence of execution to imprisonment and after a few years gave them a full pardon. In the meantime, Carr's fall led to Buckingham's rise. Thereafter gifts were showered on him. By 1618 he had joined the ranks of the peerage as Earl of Buckingham (he became duke in 1623) and James had given him royal properties to the value of £30,000. This had been forbidden in the Book of Bounty and was therefore probably illegal. It was also very unpopular. One contemporary noted sourly, 'No man danced, no man runs or jumps better, indeed he jumped higher than any Englishman did in so short a time from private gentleman to dukedom'. The fall of the Howards which followed the dismissal of Suffolk from the post of Lord Treasurer in 1618 left the field open to Buckingham. From that point until his murder ten years later, he had undisputed mastery over the court and both James and Charles were utterly reliant upon him.

The first 15 years of James's reign provided an indicator of the conflicts between crown and parliament which were to follow. The positions of the two sides were sketched in but, at this stage, there was no inevitability about the future. Relations between king and Commons could easily have been restored, as they were to be for a while in the 1620s, if the king pursued policies which met with the approval of parliament. Finance was a more serious problem which defied an easy solution. James's extravagance obscured the very real shortage faced by the crown. Up to 1618, this problem did not become acute because

James pursued a peaceful, and therefore cheap, foreign policy. Once demands for an active foreign policy became strident, there would be no leisure for such imaginative solutions to the crown's financial needs as the Great Contract. In many ways 1603-18 can be seen as a time of missed opportunities: to put royal finances on a sound footing; to establish a working relationship between James and the House of Commons; to install royal advisers in whom the nation could have confidence. You must draw your own conclusions about who should take responsibility for these failures.

Making notes on '*Domestic Politics, 1603-18*'

This chapter and the four which follow form the core of the book and detailed notes are required from all of them. In this chapter you must consider what sort of a man James I was. A complete assessment will not be possible until chapter 5 but you should have formed a preliminary impression and decided whether the descriptions given of James seem to be supported by the facts. A related question is how far the king's problems were of his own making. Why did relations between king and parliament deteriorate so fast? It is very important to have a clear view about the processes at work because it will affect the way you look at the whole period. Use the following headings and questions as a structure for your notes.

1   The Character of James
2   Problems with Finance
2.1 James's Extravagance
2.2 The Composition of Crown Finances: ordinary revenue and
     parliamentary supply
3   The Great Contract
     What were the advantages of the Contract? Why did it fail?
4   Years of Drift 1612-18
     What did Cockayne's scheme reveal about the government's
     understanding of economic matters?
5   Relations with Parliament
     Why was the House of Commons so suspicious of James?
5.1 The Union
     What effect did this have on the crown's relations with parliament?
6   Robert Carr: rise and fall
     What did James's choice of favourite show about the king?
7   The Addled Parliament
     Does the failure of the parliament reveal that there was no direction
     to government policy between 1610 and 1621?

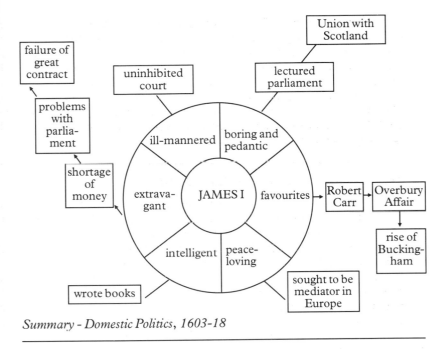

Summary - Domestic Politics, 1603-18

Source-based questions on 'Domestic Politics, 1603-18'

1 The Character of James
Carefully read the two accounts of James given on pages 23-4. Answer the following questions.
a) Identify and put into your own words the three good qualities that de Fontenay mentions. (3 marks)
b) Identify and put into your own words the three bad qualities that de Fontenay mentions. (3 marks)
c) How far can you reconcile Weldon's account with that of de Fontenay? (especially look at the second paragraph) (4 marks)
d) A 'marvellous mind' (de Fontenay, line 5), 'the wisest fool in Christendom' (Weldon, line 17), which of these two descriptions seems more accurate? Give reasons for your answer. (5 marks)

2 James's Claim to the Throne
Carefully study the family tree of James I engraved by Benjamin Wright, given on page 25. Answer the following questions.
a) Explain the double line of descent which gave James a claim to the English throne. (5 marks)
b) What is the significance of the symbol behind James and Anne? (2 marks)
c) What message is the engraving seeking to convey? (3 marks)

CHAPTER 4

Foreign Affairs, 1603-40

1 Introduction

The end of the sixteenth century brought a lull in the religious warfare which had torn Europe apart in the preceding fifty years. The only conflict which continued openly was the struggle of the Protestant United Provinces to break free from the control of Catholic Spain. This did not mean that religious strife was at an end - far from it!- but was more a product of exhaustion, and the first two decades of the seventeenth century were marked by an uneasy calm, punctuated by incidents which threatened to become major crises but were resolved. In 1618 such an incident did become a crisis with alarming speed. James's son-in-law, Frederick, Elector of the Palatinate, who was the leading German Calvinist, accepted the throne of Bohemia. The King of Bohemia was elected and the choice normally fell on a member of the Catholic Habsburgs although most of the population of Bohemia was Protestant. When the Habsburg Archduke Ferdinand became king he attempted to undermine the position of the Protestants and promote Catholics. As a result, he was deposed and Frederick was chosen in his place. Ferdinand became Emperor in 1619 and what had been a localised dispute soon plunged most of Europe into a conflict that dragged on until 1648 and became known as the Thirty Years War.

The causes of the war were complex but that there was a strong religious element is undeniable. Religion was a crucial motivating factor in foreign policy at this time. A simple formula would have been accepted by the vast majority of Englishmen in the early seventeenth century - Protestant equals good, Catholic equals bad. In any case, the sympathies of the English were already on Frederick's side because of his wife Elizabeth (she was James's daughter), and this was strengthened by the fact that he was popularly portrayed as a fervent Protestant struggling against the might of the Catholic Emperor. Many believed that England should place itself at the head of the Protestant world and fight against the forces of what they thought of as that Anti-Christ the Pope. The close link between religion and foreign policy in the popular mind was not sufficiently appreciated by either James or Charles. James was anxious to avoid war if possible and put his trust in diplomacy. He hoped that a marriage alliance with Spain would resolve the conflict because the Spanish King Philip III might be persuaded to put pressure on his cousin the Emperor. Ultimately these negotiations failed but not until Charles had made a foolish expedition in person to Madrid to try to force the issue.

The attempt to forge an alliance with a major Catholic power caused conflict with parliament and criticism of the crown's handling of foreign affairs. This criticism grew rather than diminished when Charles led the country into war against Spain in disgust at his treatment in Madrid. This was because the handling of the war was so inept. Foreign affairs were a major contributory factor in the worsening relations between Charles and the Commons which culminated in the king resolving to rule without parliament in the future. From 1629 the pursuit of solvency put an end to active interference in European affairs. England remained neutral in the 1630s despite various offers of alliances. However, increasingly Charles seemed to favour the Spanish. This foreign policy combined with the open Catholic worship of Charles's French wife, Henrietta Maria, the presence of a papal agent at court and the highly ceremonial form of worship favoured by Charles created fears of a popish plot to undermine the liberties of the country. Such fears appeared to be confirmed when the king assembled an army, not to fight in the religious war on the continent, but to impose a new prayer book on the Scots who objected to it because they felt it was semi-Catholic.

Foreign policy was an unquestioned part of the king's prerogative but when he followed aims at variance with the wishes of the vast majority of his subjects, it was bound to have major domestic repercussions. Both James and Charles failed to appreciate that their pursuit of alliances with Catholic powers would seriously affect their relations with parliament and would result in the Commons refusing to provide the finance necessary for war because they disapproved of its objectives. Foreign affairs, religion, finance and relations between king and parliament were all inter-linked. However, it is debatable whether parliament would have voted sufficient funds for the successful prosecution of a war even if they wholly approved of it. Elizabeth I had struggled in her war against Spain with the nation united behind her. Since then, military costs had risen dramatically. The king was caught in a trap. To do nothing when protestantism was under threat was unpopular but there was no certainty that there was enough money for an interventionist policy. James and Charles had difficult choices to make. Whether they made them wisely is the question this chapter addresses.

2 The Foreign Policy of James I

James was a peace lover and he was anxious above all to keep England out of a major war. He was ambitious and wished to secure a marriage alliance with the Spanish Habsburgs, still the most powerful rulers in the world. He wanted to make himself the mediator of Europe and he sought to use the marriages of his children to achieve this. At the start of the reign these three ambitions were unrealistic but not impossible. However, events were to put them all out of reach by the 1620s. The polarisation of Europe after the outbreak of the Thirty Years War produced intense pressure in the country for action to defend the Protestant cause. This put an end to the policy of peace and destroyed James's hopes of being a mediator. In any case, the Spanish marriage never stood much chance of success while the king remained committed to Protestantism, but it was useful for Spain to prolong the negotiations to prevent James from concluding a marriage alliance with a potential enemy such as France. Charles's expedition to Madrid in 1623 finally dispelled all illusions about the intentions of the Spanish.

James's reign began when war with Spain had already been dragging on for fifteen years. Both sides were anxious for peace, which was agreed in the Treaty of London in 1604. This gave English merchants the right to trade in Spain and the Spanish Netherlands without fear for their religion. The war had achieved very little for either side but now that it was over, trade could be built up again. For the next five years, James concentrated on securing his position in England and there was little participation in foreign affairs. The proposal that James should take up the leadership of a Protestant alliance, suggested in 1603, was turned down and England's only role on the continent was a limited involvement in the United Provinces' continuing struggle for independence from Spain.

In 1609 the delicate balance of Protestant and Catholic that had been established in the Holy Roman Empire (covering Germany and much of central Europe) was threatened. The Catholic ruler of the duchies of Jülich and Cleves died without a direct heir and two Protestants made claims for his lands. The Emperor sent troops to occupy the duchies which was countered by intervention from France, the United Provinces and a rather reluctant England. James would have preferred to mediate but, as events rapidly moved beyond him, he did not feel able to stand by and do nothing. In the event, the Jülich-Cleves dispute was settled peacefully by dividing the duchies, but the crisis had clearly shown that religious divisions in Germany were a major source of tension. In 1608-9 rival alliances had been set up: the Protestant Union under Frederick of the Palatinate and the Catholic League under Maximilian of Bavaria.

The Jülich-Cleves dispute had put pressure on James to give his support to the Protestant Union and this was increased after 1610 when Henry IV of France was assassinated. France was the only power strong enough to challenge the might of the Habsburgs in Spain and the Empire but Henry's heir, Louis XIII, was a child of 10 and this meant that French involvement in foreign conflicts was less likely until Louis came of age. England was the only state capable of leading the Protestant world in an anti-Habsburg alliance. In 1612 an alliance was signed between England and the Protestant Union and the following year James's daughter Elizabeth was married to Frederick of the Palatine whose family was already connected by marriage to many of the leading Protestant figures. James was now at the centre of the Protestant world.

Up to this point the king's actions had the support and approval of his non-Catholic subjects. He was pursuing a Protestant foreign policy avoiding expensive wars but seeking to contain the Habsburg threat. But after 1613 there was a change in James's policy which many people found hard to understand. He began to court the friendship of Spain and sought to promote a Catholic marriage for the heir to the throne. For those who regarded Catholics as worse than infidels, this was totally unacceptable and inexplicable. For James it was much more straightforward. He wanted a prestigious match for his son which meant either a Bourbon (French) or a Habsburg princess, and he distrusted the French. He also wished to be the peace-maker of Europe and having established his central position among the Protestants he now needed a way into the Catholic world. James was remarkably free of religious prejudice so that, although he was a convinced Protestant, he did not regard all Catholics as irretrievably damned.

From 1613, circumstances combined to give James the backing he needed to pursue a Spanish marriage and a pro-Spanish foreign policy. Philip III became anxious that England might take up leadership of a Protestant coalition, and in 1613 a new ambassador, usually known as Count Gondomar, was sent to London to win James away from the Dutch and German Protestants. He did this by offering concessions over marriage terms. Salisbury had died in 1612 and the Howard family which took control of most major offices in 1614 were pro-Spanish. Many of the Howard family were either still Catholic or were merely nominal members of the Church of England. They encouraged James to pursue a Spanish match for Charles while a rival faction at court led by the Earl of Southampton wanted an actively Protestant foreign policy. These two groups, although with many changes of personnel, would continue to divide the council until the outbreak of Civil War. The Spanish group opposed summoning parliament and encouraged the king to act on his prerogative, while the Protestant faction wanted frequent parliaments and a display of unity between king and country. This division in the council hampered the pursuit of clear objectives in the troubled years of the 1620s and encouraged those who were unhappy with the direction of the policy to seek allies in the Commons. This challenged the king's right to be solely responsible for the direction of foreign policy.

The final factor which gave the marriage negotiations some impetus was the failure of the Addled Parliament in 1614. No money had been forthcoming to satisfy the king's acute financial needs and he turned instead to the prospect of a rich Spanish dowry to make up for the shortcomings of parliament. The proposed dowry was about £600,000, which would have gone a long way to easing the king's financial difficulties. Sir John Digby was sent to Madrid to pursue negotiations although there was no great urgency because Charles was only 14 and the infanta Maria was four years younger. In the meantime, James avoided giving offence to the Spanish. One casualty of this policy was Sir Walter Raleigh. He had been kept in the Tower of London since 1603 because of his ill-considered involvement in a minor Catholic plot against James. The sentence of death which was passed at that time had not been revoked but Raleigh had not been executed and in 1617 he was released to enable him to search for gold in the region of the Orinoco River in Guiana, deep in Spanish territory. He was under strict instructions not to fight the Spanish but inevitably he did so and was therefore executed on his return in 1618.

Philip III had no real desire to marry his daughter to Charles but it suited him to keep negotiations dragging on. Into this stalemate came the bombshell of events in Prague. The Habsburg Archduke Ferdinand had been elected King of Bohemia in 1618. As his anti-Protestant attitude became apparent fears grew, and in May the nobles revoked their allegiance to him. In 1619 they offered the crown to Frederick of the Palatinate. Frederick was one of the seven electors who chose the Holy Roman Emperor. If he accepted the Bohemian crown he would gain another vote and the Protestants would be in a majority in the electoral college instead of the Catholics. This was a threat that the Habsburgs could not afford to ignore. It would alter the balance of power in central Europe and the Catholics might lose their political control of the region. Without waiting for James's advice, who was strongly against it, Frederick accepted the throne of Bohemia. He and Elizabeth took up residence in Prague but Ferdinand, who was by now Emperor, immediately moved against them. Frederick and Elizabeth became known as the Winter King and Queen because their brief reign was brought to an end at the Battle of the White Mountain in November 1620. Worse was to follow when the Palatinate was occupied by Spanish and Bavarian troops and its elector and his family were forced into exile in Holland.

These dramatic events had major repercussions in England. The fate of Frederick would have caused concern in any case but the fact that he was James's son-in-law intensified the pressure for England to act decisively on his behalf. James himself was very concerned. He thought Frederick had been extremely foolish to accept the Bohemian crown and would not help him to regain it. But he considered the Palatinate to be a very different matter. It was Frederick's hereditary land and every effort should be made to ensure he was restored as its ruler, although preferably without the use of force if possible. James pinned his hopes on the Spanish and sought to persuade them to use their influence to ensure the return of the Palatinate. James believed a settlement could be reached if the marriage treaty was achieved and the Spanish accepted his mediation. In this he was sadly mistaken. The Spanish wanted to contain the war, the conflict with the United Provinces had been resumed in 1621 and they did not want a hostile England linking up with the Dutch. They, therefore, held out the promise of a marriage while they hoped that events on the battlefield would move in their favour. From 1618 to 1623 James's policy consisted of fruitless negotiations with Spain, but he knew that the negotiations might fail to achieve their aim and that a change of policy might be forced on him. To ensure that he had funds ready to meet an emergency, parliament was summoned in 1621.

The lack of decisive action by the crown had not been popular. The general view echoed that of Archbishop Abbot:

> 1 God had set up this prince [Frederick] as a mark of honour throughout all Christendom, to propagate the gospel and to protect the oppressed ... Therefore let not a noble son be forsaken for their sakes who regard nothing but their own ends ... Therefore
> 5 let all our spirits be gathered up to animate this business, that the world may take notice that we are awake when God calls.

The Commons wanted to help Frederick, but they were not willing to vote large sums of money to be squandered by James especially as there was a trade depression and poor harvests. It was estimated that £1,000,000 a year would be needed to mount an adequate expedition to the Palatinate, which would be difficult to organise - for example how would the army be supplied?. The king took the unusual step of inviting the Commons to discuss foreign policy, which lay outside their jurisdiction, hoping that an aggressive display of hostility would put pressure on Spain to make concessions to avoid the likelihood of war. This was a risky procedure and one that needed delicate handling in the conduct of debates, if parliament's support for war was not to turn into criticism of royal policy. The Commons were asked for a speedy vote to supply but it was not clear what the money would be used for. Parliament wanted an alliance with the Dutch and a sea war against Spain. This was a less foolish option that at first appears. Spanish gold helped pay for the Imperial forces in Germany and her troops occupied the Lower Palatinate. If Spain and the Spanish Netherlands came under threat, Spanish pressure might force the Emperor into a settlement.

James had a very different strategy. He wanted to use parliament to push Spain into concessions, but if all else failed he was prepared to mount an expedition to try and win back the Palatinate directly, in alliance with the Dutch and the German princes. He did not want to break his ties with Spain because that would put an end to his hopes of negotiating a marriage treaty. Having invited the Commons to discuss foreign policy, James made the mistake of not informing them fully of his intentions. He wanted an anti-Habsburg not an anti-Catholic league because he hoped for French involvement. So he avoided mentioning religion. He was also reluctant to name the enemy as this would restrict his freedom of action. This meant that the Commons were left uncertain about the king's real intentions. In a petition they urged James 'to pursue and more publicly avow the aiding of those of our religion in foreign parts.' They wanted all negotiations with Spain to be ended. But rather than go along with this James dissolved parliament.

This abrupt termination of parliament marks the beginning of an active dislike of the crown's foreign policy that was to intensify in Charles's reign. James's behaviour seemed inexplicable. The country could not understand why a Protestant monarch should seek to marry his son to a Catholic princess whose fellow countrymen were fighting his own son-in-law's troops. This level of suspicion soured parliament's relations with the crown and left James, and subsequently Charles, deeply annoyed that the Commons would not vote sufficient funds for them to pursue an effective foreign policy. The attempt to follow an aggressive policy without adequate resources led to a number of military disasters in the 1620s and these in turn led to a worsening of relations and an unwillingness by parliament to co-operate in the future. It was a vicious circle that could be broken either by successful pursuit of an actively Protestant foreign policy or by dispensing with parliament. Since the former proved beyond him, in 1629 Charles decided to manage without parliament. Before then, however, he had a brief moment of overwhelming popularity on his return home from Madrid in 1623.

3 The Trip to Madrid

In February 1623 two young men with the unlikely names of Jack and Tom Smith set off for the Continent. When they were arrested for suspicious behaviour in Canterbury, Tom Smith had to remove his false beard to reveal that he was the Lord Admiral, the Marquess of Buckingham. His 'brother' was the heir to the throne, Prince Charles. They were on their way to Spain on a foolhardy journey that took them through France, where they visited the court in Paris. It was a journey that was full of risk from bandits or fortune hunters who might seek a ransom. James had been very reluctant to allow them to go, but when Charles and Buckingham joined forces to request something, he found it hard to resist them for long. The purpose of the journey was to demonstrate the depth of Charles's commitment to the Infanta - it could hardly be love since he had never met her. By appearing in such dramatic fashion on the Spaniards' own doorstep, he hoped to push the negotiations to a conclusion. Charles ignored all the perils of travelling across Europe with only three companions and he did not fully consider the implications of his presence at the Spanish court where he could be kept indefinitely as an effective prisoner.

The Spanish were understandably amazed when Charles presented himself in their midst and treated him with the utmost courtesy. However he was not allowed to see the object of his affections which frustrated the young prince so much that he was reduced to climbing a garden wall to catch a glimpse of her. Nor did the presence of Charles soften the Spanish line in negotiations. If anything the reverse was true, as, with Charles in Spain, they held all the trump cards as James was almost certain to agree to anything within reason in order to get him back. The Spanish did not understand the depth of commitment in England to the Protestant faith. Gondomar had reported home unrealistically that James 'was well inclined towards the Mass' and that 'everything here depends solely on the king's will, he has sufficient authority to introduce the sect of Turks or Moors if he pleases.' So the Spanish believed that if only they could win James over to their side he would be able to reconvert England with little opposition. They assumed that Charles had come to Spain to convert to Catholicism. When they realised their mistake they insisted on firm guarantees about toleration for Catholics, although Buckingham would not let Charles agree to public worship for Catholics which James had always opposed. Their terms for the restoration of the Palatinate, which was closely linked in James's mind with the marriage, were the restoration of Frederick's heir, Frederick Henry, after his conversion to Catholicism, education at the Imperial Court and marriage to a Habsburg archduchess. These were impossible terms for either James or Frederick to swallow.

As Charles and Buckingham's presence in Madrid was prolonged throughout the summer, James became anxious to get them back under any circumstances. It was now apparent that the policy of mediation had failed and that a Spanish match could only be achieved on unacceptable terms. A marriage treaty was agreed in outline but once Charles was safely away from Spanish shores it was not marriage he was thinking of but war in revenge for the humiliation of his treatment in Spain. Buckingham who had been created a duke in his absence by James - the first non-royal duke for a century and a clear sign that James regarded him as one of the family - was equally keen to go to war. The main obstacle was the king who was still opposed to involvement in European conflict. However, he was unable to withstand the combined pressure of his son, his favourite and the country.

4 Moves to War

When Charles and Buckingham returned home from Spain in October 1623 they were met with scenes of tumultuous rejoicing, 'the loudest and most universal of the whole kingdom that the nation had ever been acquainted with'. One contemporary counted no less than 335 bonfires between Whitehall and Temple Bar in the City of London. The people felt that their prince had been restored to them, he was alive and still a Protestant. In the polarised conditions of the 1620s it was difficult for an important power such as England to maintain a neutral stance for long. To avoid war which had been James's policy up to 1623 was in effect to help the Catholic side. When Charles and Buckingham returned, eager for revenge on Spain, the only way this could be adequately expressed was by declaring war and this was enormously popular in the country which had been waiting in vain for a distinctly Protestant lead from

James. The first step was to call parliament to vote funds for a war. James was reluctant to do so but he was ill in November 1623 and could not impose his will on the two determined young men. From this point, until his death in March 1625, James found it increasingly difficult to direct events in opposition to Charles and Buckingham, although he was ready to point out to them the folly of their actions when he thought it appropriate.

James was not the only obstacle in the path of war. Several members of the Privy Council favoured a pro-Spanish policy and believed that war would be disastrous. Foremost among these was the treasurer Cranfield, Earl of Middlesex, who had been a client of Buckingham's but who now opposed the favourite's policy because of its damaging effect on the crown finances. Buckingham wanted to remove Cranfield and he used parliament and the ancient weapon of impeachment (see page 68) to have him accused of corruption. This was a dangerous policy because it invited parliament to involve itself in the choice of the king's ministers. Impeachment was a powerful weapon against men who promoted unpopular policies as Buckingham would find out to his cost in 1626 and 1628.

The parliament which met in 1624 made a pleasing exception to the usual record of suspicion and mistrust which affected the other parliaments of the early Stuarts. Harmony appeared to reign as the Commons expressed its delight at the safe return of its prince and its pleasure that war was to be declared against the arch-enemy, Spain. They voted £300,000 for this and Charles attended debates in the Upper House, well pleased with the level of support. However, this show of solidarity between Crown and Commons was deceptive. The Commons were clear that they wanted a sea war of diversion against Spain which would be partly self-financing through the capture of Spanish prizes. They did not want the uncertainty and expense of a continental war and the subsidy was therefore voted on the specific understanding that it would be used for the navy and to help the Dutch and not to mount an expedition to the Palatinate.

Buckingham had other ideas. He wanted a grand anti-Habsburg alliance. To be successful this would require the co-operation of France which could also provide a wife of sufficient status for Charles. It was also only in alliance with France that James would contemplate military action. The fact that this would send confusing messages to the country about the depth of commitment to the Protestant cause was unfortunate. But, if the strategy of encircling the Habsburgs was successful, Buckingham would be vindicated. Negotiations were begun for a marriage treaty and also for a joint Anglo-French expedition from French territory to the Palatinate. In expectation of French military assistance, Buckingham was prepared to make concessions over religion to the French that he had considered unacceptable the previous year in Spain. In the marriage treaty, signed in November 1624, it was agreed that Henrietta Maria, the French princess, her children and servants would be allowed to practise their religion freely and to have a chapel in London open to the public served by 28 priests and one bishop. Her children were to be educated as Catholics until they were 13 and Catholics were to be granted toleration. The treaty did not mention a military alliance. These extraordinary terms were extracted from Buckingham by Louis XIII's new chief minister, Cardinal Richelieu, who had no intention of making war on the Habsburgs until it suited his own purposes. Buckingham had made all the concessions and had gained nothing in return. He had become too heavily committed to withdraw from negotiations and had therefore accepted a treaty that he must have known would cause outrage in England. The crown again appeared less than whole-hearted about the Protestant cause.

All might have been forgiven if the Anglo-French expedition had been a success but at the last moment Louis refused to send any troops or to allow the expedition to cross French territory. The expedition set off under its leader, an experienced German mercenary, Count Mansfeld, in January 1625, but it immediately met with disaster. The troops were poorly equipped and the Dutch countryside where they landed had already been stripped bare by a previous army. Many of the soldiers died of disease and the rest melted away through desertion. The expedition achieved nothing, but over £60,000 of the Commons subsidy had been wasted in express defiance of their instructions.

Another part of Buckingham's strategy was to gain Protestant allies in northern Europe. In 1624 James agreed to finance 6,000 English troops for two years to fight in the Netherlands' war of independence. In February 1625 it was arranged with Denmark that England would pay for 7,000 troops at a cost of £30,000 per month in return for a Danish campaign in Germany. This was a way of helping the Protestant cause while avoiding war but it required considerable finance which would have to come from parliament. The Commons had already made clear that it did not want to subsidise foreign allies and it disliked this use of parliamentary funds. The conduct of the war was already proving controversial. At this point James died. The new king, Charles, did not share his father's aversion to war and was anxious to play a full part in the struggle against the Habsburgs and to secure the restoration of his brother-in-law. James had prevented the declaration of war against Spain but nothing now prevented a grand naval strategy except a lack of finance. The 1624 parliament had shown itself sympathetic to Charles and Buckingham's policies and so writs for a new parliament were issued the day after James died.

5 War against Spain

Charles and his chief minister were under the illusion that the 1625 parliament would be as co-operative as its predecessor and that it was not necessary to arrange for spokesmen to explain crown policy to the Commons. This ignored how the intervening events appeared to parliamentary eyes. No war had been declared against Spain, a marriage alliance had been made with France that seemed to promote Catholicism in England, a disastrous expedition had been sent to the continent against the terms of the 1624 subsidy, and expensive undertakings had been made to European allies. It was with some justification that the Commons wondered who exactly the enemy was. They doubted the king's commitment to the Protestant cause and they wanted firm guarantees about how any war would be conducted. There were also domestic grievances, above all the relaxation of the recusancy laws against Catholics which had accompanied Charles's marriage to Henrietta Maria in May. Charles's request for an immediate grant and a postponement of debate on domestic matters therefore fell on deaf ears. All that the Commons would offer to relieve the crown's pressing financial need was two subsidies worth £140,000. This decision was justified on the grounds that no war had been declared and there had been no account given of the money voted in 1624. It was suggested that if the fleet returned successfully there might be a better incentive to grant supply. This situation infuriated the king, who felt that parliament was refusing to finance a war to which it had agreed. He made the unprecedented request for more money to be granted by the same session but this merely served to unite the Commons against him. When parliament attacked Buckingham, Charles dissolved it in August 1625.

The king was left with many expensive foreign undertakings and not enough money to pay for them. The most immediate need was for fitting-out the navy which was assembling in Plymouth for an expedition against Spain. The navy and its accompanying army were both in a very poor state, requiring food and clothing. Some of the provisions which had been purchased had already gone rotten but there was no money for more. At the end of August, the Treasurer revealed that there was only £600 left in the exchequer and it would not be replenished until the first subsidy payments started to come in during October. The queen's dowry of £120,000 had been used on the expedition and Charles borrowed £70,000 from an international financier to enable it to set sail. Altogether about half a million pounds had been spent getting the expedition ready but it was still short of many essentials. It was over twenty years since a fleet of this size had been needed and the administrative system could not cope with the complexity of the task. The fleet set sail in October and landed near Cadiz. As the soldiers advanced to attack the town they came across a farm full of vats of wine. The soldiers got drunk and the expedition degenerated into a farce. The attack was abandoned, an attempt to intercept the Plate fleet failed, and sickness swept through the ships as they ran short of beer and water. The fleet crept home in humiliation. It had achieved nothing at enormous cost and Buckingham who was Lord Admiral received much of the blame, not entirely fairly because he had worked hard to get adequate provisions for the expedition. Undeterred, he and Charles pressed on with further military preparations. Charles even pawned the crown jewels to raise money while Buckingham continued to push for a general anti-Habsburg League. The key to his strategy was the co-operation of France.

6 Relations with France

Buckingham needed the help of France to mount an effective campaign against the Habsburgs. However, he was no match for the wily Richelieu who used Buckingham to gain his own objectives against the Huguenots (French Protestants), without having any intention of joining against the Habsburgs until he was certain that it was in France's best interests to do so. In September 1625 England and the United Provinces signed the treaty of Southampton which bound them together in an offensive and defensive alliance. France and others were invited to join this league but only Denmark accepted and the treaty of The Hague was signed in December. Charles agreed to pay Christian IV, King of Denmark, £30,000 a month for his army and undertook to prepare a second fleet to which the Dutch would contribute some ships.

The refusal of France to attend the discussions at The Hague created suspicions about its trustworthiness. There had already (in September 1625) been a highly embarrassing incident for Buckingham when English ships on loan to France were used to defeat a Huguenot force off La Rochelle. This had caused an outrage because the Huguenots were fellow Protestants whom the king had a moral duty to defend and Charles had made repeated attempts to secure the return of the ships. The royal marriage had not begun well. Charles and Henrietta Maria were barely on speaking terms and there was friction over the size of her household and especially over the number of priests she had brought with her. The final example of French untrustworthiness came in February 1626. Just as Buckingham was hoping that the French could be persuaded to join the war effort, they made a separate peace with Spain at Monzon.

Buckingham was furious and decided that he must engineer the removal of Richelieu before there could be any hope of changing French policy. He made contact with members of the French aristocracy who also wished to remove the Cardinal and determined on a three pronged attack with the Huguenots and the Dukes of Lorraine and Savoy. An English fleet would be sent to begin the uprising which would link up with the Huguenots. Parliamentary finance would be required to prepare this fleet. In the meantime relations between England and France steadily deteriorated as first Henrietta Maria's household was expelled and then each country began seizing the other's shipping.

The parliament of 1626 was not impressed with the fruits of the duke's foreign policy. So far they had seen negotiations with Catholic powers which had brought little to England but had involved concessions over religion and the loan of English ships. Two military expeditions had been sent out. The first under Mansfeld, which had been in violation of the subsidy act, had failed miserably and the second to Cadiz had been a hugely expensive fiasco. On the continent, the Protestant cause was going badly. After April 1626 only the Danes were left in the field to face the full might of the imperial armies. Parliament was willing to back the king's foreign policy but only if he would remove Buckingham and this was the one thing Charles would not do. The parliament of 1626 was dissolved without a subsidy being granted but the needs were as great as ever. In January 1627 the workers in the dockyard at Chatham, who had received no pay for a year, marched to London to demand their arrears, and work came to a halt until £8,000 could be found. Charles decided to levy a forced loan from his richer subjects to supply the funds that parliament would have voted if it had not been dissolved.

In October 1626 another fleet set sail for Spain, not because it was ready, but because so much money had already been spent on it and it could not be maintained over the winter. The supplies which had been assembled with such difficulty would go rotten and it would be impossible to prevent large numbers of the sailors from deserting. This time the expedition failed even to reach the coast of Spain. It was struck by violent storms in the Bay of Biscay and had to return home. It seemed that England was incapable of mounting a successful attack against one country, yet the Duke of Buckingham was preparing to go to war against France as well.

7 War with France

Buckingham's policy in relation to France was quite straightforward. He wrote about Habsburg domination:

> It is clear that if the powers act one by one they will but destroy themselves. All must conspire for one end. If France, which is the vital part of this body, fails us, it will be proper to harass her, so that if she refuses to do good she may be prevented from doing harm.

Relations with France had steadily deteriorated over the winter of 1626-7. The tit-for-tat seizures of shipping culminated in the capture of the English wine fleet at Bordeaux which incensed the nation. This was hypocritical because it was the capture of French prizes that provided ready money for the navy to be equipped. Buckingham also spent £10,000 of his own money on the expedition but the bulk of the finance had to come from the forced loan which met with considerable resistance.

By June 1627 everything was ready and Buckingham resolved to lead the expedition in person. The plan was to capture the island of Rhé which guarded the approach to La Rochelle, the Huguenot stronghold, and by so doing, to encourage a general uprising by the Huguenots which would link with separate attacks by the Dukes of Lorraine and Savoy. It was hoped that this would either bring about Richelieu's downfall or force him to change his policy. At first things went well. Troops were landed on the island and its citadel was besieged. But then it all began to go wrong. Buckingham showed great courage and determination but he was inexperienced in military affairs. He did not receive adequate backing from England so that necessary supplies and reinforcements, which had been promised, failed to arrive. The final disaster was when the scaling ladders for storming the citadel were found to be too short and the expedition returned in November having achieved nothing.

Buckingham should not be blamed for the failure of the attack, but he bore the major responsibility for the policy which had led to it. The English administration had proved incapable of sustaining a war effort. New systems of credit were needed if military operations were not to be continually halted by a shortage of cash. As armies became larger and more sophisticated in their equipment, more effort was needed to fit out an expedition and the structures had not been developed to do this efficiently. So one disaster followed another throughout the 1620s and the English people were in no doubt about who should be blamed. One contemporary noted that Buckingham's 'coming safe home occasioned almost as much sorrow as the slaughter and perishing of all the rest.'

The failure of the expedition to Rhé resolved nothing and in some ways made matters worse. France and Spain agreed in principle upon a combined attack on England which fortunately came to nothing, but it did necessitate further military preparations to defend the country. In Germany the Danes, let down by the failure of England to fulfil its promise of money, were beaten by imperial forces and Christian IV was forced to retreat back into Denmark and to withdraw from the war. The Huguenots were requesting aid and the forces of Protestantism were apparently in retreat across the continent.

An expedition to relieve La Rochelle, under siege by Louis's troops, was sent out in the spring of 1628. This was led by Buckingham's brother-in-law, the Earl of Denbigh, and was an even more miserable failure than previous undertakings. Parliament was in session when the expedition returned and it fuelled a parliamentary crisis. Feelings were already running high about the forced loan and the billeting of troops for the various expeditions and there was a determination to put an end to these grievances through their prohibition and to remove the Duke of Buckingham. One wit wrote about him in 1628:

And now, just God! I humbly pray
That thou wilt take that slime away
That keeps my sovereign's eyes from viewing
The things that will be our undoing!

Foreign policy poisoned Charles's relations with his first three parliaments as the apparent lack of direction at the start of the reign gave way to bungled military expeditions at appalling expense. Parliament was unwilling to vote large sums of money only to see them frittered away without anything being achieved. The lack of adequate finance drove the king to find money by whatever means he could even if this created further conflict with parliament. He continued to collect tonnage and poundage throughout the reign, although it had been sanctioned for only the first year; troops were billeted on unwilling households to cut the cost of their upkeep; and, most important of all, when parliament refused to grant a subsidy unless the Duke of Buckingham was removed, Charles extracted a forced loan to the amount of five subsidies. Insufficient funds had an inevitable result on the success of foreign enterprises. In the circumstances it was a great achievement for Buckingham to equip three naval expeditions by early 1628 without the usual backing of parliamentary finance. However, it was not only lack of money which caused failure. Another serious shortcoming was the quality of the commanders and of the men they were supposed to be leading. The soldiers and sailors who went on these expeditions tended to be from the lowest levels of society - criminals and vagrants, ill-equipped and ill-trained. Only an inspired leader could make much of them and the leaders who were chosen (Sir Edward Cecil, Buckingham and the Earl of Denbigh) proved incapable of motivating them.

Two men who were to play a significant part in the history of the late 1620s were officers on the Cadiz expedition and were appalled by what they saw. One, Sir John Eliot, had been a client of Buckingham's but became convinced that the favourite was incapable of sustaining a war. He became prominent in the parliamentary opposition and did much to turn the Commons against the king's policy. In 1626 he declared:

Our honour is ruined, our ships are sunk; our men perished; not by the sword, not by the enemy, not by chance, but, as the strongest predictions had discerned and made it appeared beforehand, by those we trust.

The other man who was disillusioned by the Cadiz expedition was Lieutenant John Felton. In the summer of 1628 Buckingham was in Plymouth supervising the preparation of yet another expedition to La Rochelle when he was fatally stabbed by Felton.

The nation rejoiced while Charles mourned for his friend. At first he was determined to carry on with Buckingham's policy and the expedition in Plymouth set out in the autumn with the same sorry results as before. La Rochelle fell to the forces of the French king and there seemed little point in pursuing the war. An additional impetus towards peace came from Charles's decision to rule without parliament. Peace was made with France in the treaty of Suza in April 1629 which was a tacit agreement to bury the past. Peace with Spain took longer to achieve but in November 1630 the treaty of Madrid was signed. This was essentially a repeat of the 1604 treaty of London but Philip IV gave a written promise that he would agree to the restoration of the Palatinate as part of a general settlement.

What had the foreign policy of the 1620s achieved? Obviously very little that was positive. The results of active involvement on the Continent were negligible, except in the disillusion of allies like Denmark and the Huguenots who had relied on English promises of assistance. The domestic cost of the foreign escapades of the 1620s was quite appalling. An empty treasury, a nation divided by the forced loan, relations between the king and his parliament that had become so bad that he had decided to rule without it, and a feeling of national dishonour at the performance of English forces. The hopes of glory and the desire to further the Protestant cause had all come to nothing. Who was to blame? Parliament thought it was Buckingham's fault and Charles condemned the Commons for not providing finance. The truth is that both must accept responsibility. Buckingham made some disastrous mistakes in diplomacy, especially in his dealings with France. He did his best to ensure that the expeditions were adequately equipped but he was not a natural leader and the choice of other commanders was poor. Parliament, full of suspicion about the direction of affairs, refused to grant any realistic subsidies for the war and drove Charles to adopt policies which increased the rift between them. In brief, it was not a happy story!

8 Foreign Affairs in the Personal Rule

The ending of the war against Spain brought England's active involvement in continental affairs to an end. If Charles was to rule for a sustained period without parliament he needed to balance his books and avoid expensive foreign undertakings. This did not mean a complete end to foreign diplomacy. England's alliance, or at least benevolent neutrality, was still a prize worth pursuing in war-torn Europe.

As the 1630s progressed Charles increasingly favoured Spain. In 1635 he is reported to have said 'the Spaniards are my friends on whom I can rely. All the rest is deception and villainy'. Spain was anxious to woo England away from the Anglo-Dutch alliance which caused them considerable difficulties: in 1628 for example, the Dutch had captured the entire Spanish treasure fleet with bullion worth about £1.2 million.

If Spain could secure English neutrality on terms favourable to itself, it could wage war against the Dutch much more effectively. In late 1630, proposals were made to Charles for Anglo-Spanish naval co-operation at the expense of the Dutch. Spanish ships captured by the Dutch were seized in English ports and allowed to return to Spain, and privateers from Dunkirk (then part of the Spanish Netherlands) were able to shelter and refit in Britain thus enabling them to attack Dutch ships more safely and effectively. This was a reversal of the previous policy which had favoured the Dutch and was especially damaging to the Dutch West India Company whose ships needed the protection of British ports as they returned to the Netherlands.

This policy caused considerable unease in the country which was still anxious to help the Protestant cause despite the failures of the 1620s. In 1631 a new opportunity to secure the return of the Palatinate was provided by the triumph of the Swedish army at Breitenfeld. The Swedish king, Gustavus Adolphus, was prepared to commit his forces to the restoration of the Palatinate but only if Charles would give him £200,000 in military aid. Such a cause was popular in the country and parliament would probably have been willing to grant the necessary sums. Much of the council and the queen favoured re-opening the war and the decision not to call a parliament was a turning point in Charles's reign. This was an opportunity for the king to demonstrate that, despite the misunderstandings of the past, he was definitely committed to the Protestant cause. It might even have helped soften the impact of the religious changes he was introducing which restored ritual and ceremony to church services and which appeared popish to many. Instead, Charles turned his back on parliamentary politics to pursue a course that caused distress and incomprehension in the country. Spain was allowed to mint silver in England and ships were provided to carry it across to Spanish forces in the Netherlands. By the end of the 1630s men as well as money were being carried in English ships.

This assistance to Spain was matched by the arrival of a papal agent at court in 1635, the open Catholicism of Henrietta Maria and her entourage, and Charles's willingness to negotiate with the Pope on the grounds that 'as the Pope is a temporal prince, we shall not be unwilling to join with him, as we do with other Catholic Roman Princes, in anything that may conduce to the peace of Christendom and the Church'. All this gave credence to the idea of a popish plot - that Charles was planning to convert the country by force using Spanish or Irish troops. It is a measure of either Charles's lack of skill or of his aloofness from public opinion that he did not appreciate the level of dissatisfaction his policies had caused. When a pro-Spanish foreign policy was linked to introducing a form of Anglicanism which seemed Catholic in many aspects the result was that many were suspicious of the court and all it seemed to stand for. Charles was sincere in desiring the return of the Palatinate, but it was less important to him than a Spanish alliance or the rejection of parliament. The Thirty Years War dragged on to its conclusion in 1648 but England played no part in restoring the Lower Palatinate to Frederick Henry, the son of Frederick. By then civil war was tearing the country apart, brought on partly by fear of the king's intentions towards religion as they seemed to be revealed by his foreign policy.

9 Conclusion

James I and Charles I both pursued friendship with Spain for much of their reigns to the detriment of their relations with the nation and especially with parliament. In the early part of James's reign - up to about 1614 - the king's commitment to the Protestant cause was not in doubt, although there were only minor incidents to put it to the test. The only period when England pursued an actively Protestant foreign policy was when the Duke of Buckingham was in charge after 1623. Unfortunately the wars against France and Spain were mishandled so badly that nothing came of them, and the parliaments were badly managed so that instead of willingly granting money, they imposed conditions including, above all, the replacement of Buckingham. The Commons failed to appreciate the level of funding that would be required to wage war successfully and the sums it voted even when it supported crown policy were hopelessly inadequate. Charles could not forgive this refusal to finance a war that he believed parliament had approved in 1624, even though the war that was actually fought was very different from that envisaged by the Commons who had wanted a diversionary naval war against Spain - not three expeditions to France. All over Europe, rulers were finding that the financing of warfare was difficult and put strains on the loyalty of their subjects. England was unusual only in possessing a vigorous representative institution that could withstand the pressure to tax ever more heavily. But if war was expensive and therefore potentially unpopular, avoiding war was often regarded as even worse. This was the dilemma facing the Stuart kings. There would always be problems whatever foreign policy was chosen. Unfortunately after about 1622, James and Charles seemed to have had a genius for making the worst choices. The foreign policy of the personal rule helped to create a climate of suspicion about the king's intentions and fuelled fears of a popish conspiracy to seize control of the country. This led to a breakdown of trust between Charles and his subjects which made future reconciliation much harder to achieve.

Making notes on 'Foreign Affairs, 1603-40'

There is a lot of detail in this chapter and it can be difficult knowing what to put in and what to leave out. One way of tackling this problem is to make a chronological table of the main events with a minimum of detail so that you have a good idea of what happened when. It is not necessary to learn every minor incident - you are concentrating on the overall shape of affairs. Now comes the interesting part! Having established the sequence of events it is time to look at their significance. Ask yourself the following questions:
i)   Was the Stuarts' foreign policy misguided, especially in relation to Spain?
ii) What effect did foreign affairs have on domestic politics?
iii) Was foreign policy and its conduct the main reason for the breakdown of relations with parliament in the 1620s?
iv) Would an altered policy have made a substantial difference to the reign of Charles I?

You might be able to use the above questions to provide the headings for your notes on the chapter. If you do, they will help to focus your mind on the issues rather than the detail. But this kind of note-taking requires practice and if it seems easier to answer the questions after you have made notes that will work just as well. Use the headings in the chapter to help you.

Answering essay questions on 'Foreign Affairs, 1603-40'

There is no reason why essay questions on foreign affairs should not cover the whole period but, in practice, examiners tend to concentrate on more specific areas. Study the following questions.
1   How wise were the policies which James I adopted towards Spain?
2   Why did England go to war with both Spain and France between 1625 and 1630, and what were the results?
3   What was the effect of the Thirty Years War on English foreign policy?
4   Why, and with what justification, was James I's foreign policy criticised?
5   Explain how Charles I's foreign policy contributed to the growth of opposition to the crown.
6   How would you defend James I's foreign policy?
7   'The best he could afford'. Is this a fair judgement on the overseas policy of Charles I between 1625 and 1640?

Group the questions according to their subject matter. You will see that

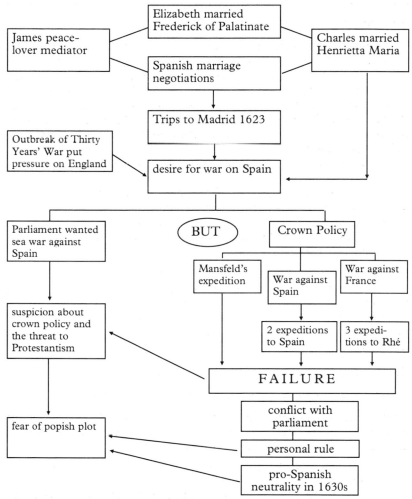

Summary - Foreign Affairs, 1603-40

questions 1, 4 and 6 go together as do questions 2 and 3 while questions 5 and 7 cover part of the same ground as questions 2 and 3 but also extend into the 1630s. Questions 4 and 6 are essentially the same question looked at from a slightly different perspective and both they and question 1 require you to make your own assessment about the direction of James's foreign policy. Question 7 does the same for Charles. They do not lend themselves to a purely descriptive treatment (or narrative as it is often called) and therefore are good types of question to attempt, especially if you feel the need of a framework to organise your thoughts.

The danger with questions 2,3 and 5 is that it would be very easy to give a simple description of what happened with no real argument (or analysis). These questions are superficially tempting because they look easy, but in order to score high marks you need to construct an argument with opposing points of view. To answer question 2, draw up a list of the reasons why England went to war and another list of the disadvantages of such a policy. Then note down the results, both domestic and foreign. You should now be able to write an essay setting out the arguments for and against war and why the war party triumphed, which will lead into consideration of the results.

A full answer to question 5 will not be possible until you have studied chapters 5 and 7 because you would need to link opposition to foreign policy into the wider picture of opposition to many aspects of domestic policy. Remember that, although the period has been divided up into domestic politics, religion and foreign policy, there was no such division in reality and essay questions will reflect this, so many will cross the boundaries between one category and another.

Source-based questions on 'Foreign Affairs, 1603-40'

1 Archbishop Abbot on English involvement in the Thirty Years' War

Carefully read Archbishop Abbot's reasons why England should become involved in the Thirty Years War, given on page 45. Answer the following questions.

a) What do you understand by the phrase 'propagate the gospel' (line 2)? (2 marks)

b) In what ways does Archbishop Abbot's view of foreign policy differ from that of James? (4 marks)

c) Why did Abbot's view put pressure on the king? (4 marks)

2 Buckingham and Foreign Affairs

Carefully read the extract by Buckingham on page 52 and then those on page 54 which criticised the Duke. Answer the following questions.

a) How convincing is Buckingham's logic for an attack on France? (4 marks)

b) How does Eliot's choice of words and phrasing help to make his point more effectively? (3 marks)

c) Do you think the verse against Buckingham or Eliot's attack upon him in the House of Commons would be more effective at rousing public opinion against the Duke? Give reasons for your answer. (5 marks)

d) In your opinion, does the first extract justify the tone of the second two? Explain your answer. (3 marks)

CHAPTER 5

Domestic Politics, 1618-29

From 1618 to 1629 the Duke of Buckingham dominated the government of England with dire results for harmony between king and Commons. Buckingham won the hearts of both James and Charles and as the 1620s progressed he exercised increasing control over the direction of policy and the distribution of patronage. In the process he became the most hated man in the kingdom and his assassination in 1628 was greeted with great joy. At first Charles tried to continue his policies, especially in foreign affairs, but these required large sums of money and, after a series of difficult encounters, Charles had become disillusioned with parliaments. A final stormy session in 1629 led to his resolving to rule without them, thus ending the first period of his reign.

The dominance of the duke helped to disguise the real differences that existed between James, who died in March 1625, and Charles. There was an obvious change in style: Charles was much more formal and dignified than his father. But it was in their attitude to their subjects that a serious difference lay. James was theatrical in manner. He liked to lecture about his divine status and he appreciated gestures of submissiveness, as when the Commons stood bare-headed to receive a message in 1621. But he knew how to negotiate and when to concede a point. Charles was much more withdrawn and he regarded any opposition to his wishes as at best mistaken and at worst as treasonable. He was prepared to be gracious in victory but only if those who opposed him would acknowledge the error of their ways and throw themselves on his mercy. The Commons was used to debating matters with the sovereign in a more open and robust manner and it was not prepared to learn this new technique.

When there were conflicts between sovereign and parliaments, it was traditional (and safer) to put the blame on evil counsellors. The major issue of the 1620s was foreign policy and, as we saw in the last chapter, there were substantial differences of opinion between king and parliament about the direction of foreign affairs. From 1625 there were also fears about religion as Charles began to promote Arminians to positions of influence within the Church. These differences were made more acute by the king's pressing need for money which gave the Commons a strong bargaining position and enabled them to attack Charles's ministers whose advice they believed was leading him astray. At first the attack was directed at members of the government whom the king regarded as dispensable - Lord Chancellor Bacon in 1621 and Lord Treasurer Cranfield in 1624 - but then there was no one left to blame except the Duke of Buckingham. Attacks on Buckingham were intensified from 1625 and made relations between Charles and parliament much worse than might otherwise have been the case. Let us look more closely at the man whose influence upon English history seems to have been totally malign despite the fact that personally he had a number of good qualities.

1 The Duke of Buckingham

George Villiers, who was born in 1592, was the second son of a second marriage of a minor member of the Leicestershire gentry. He would normally have had little chance for advancement. However, in the event, his rise was spectacular and possibly unprecedented. In 1626 the Commons issued Articles of Impeachment against Buckingham which included a list of his titles and offices.

1 George, Duke, Marquis and Earl of Buckingham, Earl of
  Coventry, Viscount Villiers, Baron of Whaddon, Great Admiral of
  the   kingdoms of England and Ireland, and of the principality of
  Wales ... general governor of the seas and ships of the said
5 kingdom, Lieutenant-general, Admiral, Captain-general and
  Governor of his Majesty's royal fleet and army lately set forth,
  Master of the Horse of our Sovereign Lord the King, Lord
  Warden, Chancellor and Admiral of the Cinque Ports, and of the
  members thereof, Constable of Dover Castle, Justice in Eyre of the
10 forests and chases on this side of the river Trent, Constable of the
  Castle of Windsor, Gentleman of his Majesty's bedchamber, one
  of his Majesty's most honourable Privy Council in his realms both
  in England, Scotland and Ireland, and knight of the most
  honourable order of the Garter.

It is perhaps not surprising that one of the charges against Buckingham was the engrossing (accumulating) of offices. Indeed, it was his monopoly of patronage and closeness to James and Charles which was the most harmful aspect of his power. By excluding other counsels from consideration by the king he distorted the system of government. As the 1620s progressed the Privy Council lost its importance as the forum for discussion and advice to the king. This engendered feelings of powerlessness amongst those who wished to pursue other courses and encouraged them to push for their policies in parliament, especially in the Commons. In 1626 one MP moved that

the cause of all the grievances is that all the king's Council ride upon one horse, therefore the parliament shall advise the king to take unto him assistants.

Charles ignored this suggestion but he paid the price of having his policies criticised in parliament by those such as Sir Thomas Wentworth who wished to join the royal government and felt excluded.

Buckingham has received a generally bad press from historians.

George Villiers, 1st Duke of Buckingham. Attributed to W. Larkim c. 1616

These quotations from Conrad Russell are typical,

1 one of the most corrupt ministers the crown has ever had . . .
Buckingham must have had talents: no man without talent could
have succeeded in descending as favourite from father to son. But
talent for devising policies or conducting administration was not
5 among Buckingham's abilities.

More recently there has been a much more sympathetic appraisal of the
duke by Roger Lockyer who, in a major biography, has sought to place
him in his context. Everyone has commented on the duke's
extravagance which mirrored that of James. On an income of £20,000 in
the 1620s he still managed to run up debts which stood at £70,000 when

he died. But Lockyer points out that power was, in part, demonstrated by conspicuous consumption. When Buckingham spent £3,000 a year on clothes, a phenomenal sum, he was advertising his great wealth which was a sign of his status. There was also an expectation, which would not have affected a lesser man, that all services would be financially rewarded however trivial they were. Buckingham's life consisted of an endless distribution of largesse to those who waited upon him or with whom he came into contact. Contemporaries were less understanding. They wanted the king's favour distributed more evenly and believed that if Buckingham's expenditure was curbed the crown's financial position would improve. In reality the crown's financial problems were too serious to be solved by restraining grants to Buckingham, although such restraint would have been an important symbolic gesture.

In James's reign, Buckingham never achieved total power because the old king retained some influence over his actions. Buckingham was only 22 when he came to the king's notice in 1614 and he had much to learn. As he grew in power, his patronage extended to a wide range of people so that he favoured both the financial reformer Lionel Cranfield and the Puritan John Preston. This meant that contrasting viewpoints still received a hearing at court. After James's death, Charles, who was bored by administration, increasingly left the direction of business to Buckingham, although he retained control over the direction of overall policy. Stories began to circulate that the duke was the real ruler and that when they went to play tennis at St. James's, Buckingham rode in a carriage while the king walked at his side, a reversal of what should happen. After 1625 Buckingham moved away from the Puritans and favoured Arminians (see page 95). This seemed suspicious when combined with lax enforcement of the laws against Catholics. Buckingham's control of the armed forces prompted fears that he was intending to seize control of the government and establish a Catholic state. The Commons identified Buckingham as the source of all its concern and it refused to work with Charles while the Duke was in office. The government was kept short of the finances it needed to protect the country from invasion and Charles felt compelled to take prerogative measures to raise money which confirmed the worst suspicions of the Commons. Buckingham's death did not solve any problems. Harmony was not restored between king and commons and finance and religion continued to drive them apart. The ecstatic scenes of joy when news of his murder came out were misplaced. Charles became even more remote from his people and shut himself off within the confines of his court and the 1630s saw the implementation of increasingly unpopular policies without the shield of a chief minister who could be blamed.

In 1618 this was a long way in the future. Buckingham was a young man who had come to prominence with the backing of a group of reformers. The king's finances were in a desperate state and the favourite gave support to a London merchant who held out the promise of improvement.

2 Cranfield and the King's Finances

The most pressing task facing the government in 1618 was to try and repair the damage done to crown finances by the lord treasurership of the Earl of Suffolk. One obvious solution was to use the expertise of city financiers. Lionel Cranfield was an astute businessman who had made large sums for himself through his dealings in trade and as part of a syndicate that had won the customs farm. He was anxious to gain entry into royal service and had acted as Buckingham's financial adviser. Buckingham, in turn, promoted him at court. James I later said Cranfield

> made so many projects for my profit that Buckingham fell in liking with him ... and brought him to my service ... He found this man so studious for my profit that he backed him against great personages and mean, without sparing of any man.

The Council was determined to cut expenditure and made Cranfield Master of the Wardrobe. This department was costing £42,000 a year and Cranfield was appointed on the understanding that if costs fell below £20,000, he could keep any additional savings. This figure was quickly surpassed and Cranfield made a profit of over £7,000 a year. He achieved similar success in the Household, down by £18,000 from £77,000, the Ordnance (£34,000 to £14,000) and the Navy (£53,000 to £30,000). These economies were achieved by attacking waste (such as insisting that candles were used more than once), by accurate budgeting and accounting, and by eliminating corrupt and unnecessary officials.

Careful housekeeping helped reduce the crown's expenditure but there was a limit to the savings that could be made. Major economies could only be achieved by further attacking the vested interests of crown officials - their corruption and perquisites. This would inevitably create opposition especially as Cranfield did not want wholesale reform because he himself benefited from the system as it was. His aim was to restrict the rewards of office to a much smaller circle of which he was a member.

In 1621 Cranfield was created Lord Treasurer as the Earl of Middlesex. At his installation it was said that 'if any man living can improve the king's revenue with skill and diligence, you are that good husband'. He was to need all his administrative skills and energy to tackle the task in front of him. When he became treasurer the royal finances were in a desperate state. The country was experiencing a severe depression, crown revenue had fallen while its expenditure had risen. The debt stood at £900,000, interest payments were not being met and credit was hard to obtain. Pensions were eatin up one-sixth of revenue but the king was continuing to make provision for the numerous members of the Villiers family. Cranfield attempted to control the flow of royal generosity. A new Book of Bounty (see page 27) was issued in 1619, and in 1621 he demanded an immediate stop to the payment of pensions and insisted that new grants should be screened by himself. This system could only have worked with the full co-operation of the king, but although James promised that he would not 'make every day Christmas' he found it impossible to resist the greed of his courtiers. He once burst out 'You will never let me alone. I would to God you had, first my doublet, and then my shirt; and when I were naked, I think you would give me leave to be quiet'. Any new source of revenue immediately increased demands on the king. The worst offender of all was Buckingham. One example will show why the crown's finances would not improve while the court was filled with men like him. A new imposition was put on coal and Cranfield made an agreement with the customs farmers that they would pay £16,000 to the crown, but he was instructed that 'His Majesty told me that £8,000 must be for my lord Admiral'. Half of the increase in duty went to enrich not the King but Buckingham. Courtiers knew that if they could present their demands directly to James, he could be persuaded to over-rule any restrictions on his power to make gifts.

Cranfield only survived as Lord Treasurer for two and a half years and the number of enemies he made is proof partly of his difficult personality but also of his drive and determination. Existing sources of revenue were exploited more effectively but he failed in an attempt to reduce pensions and end the practice whereby men would sell or bequeath them to others. He refused to sell crown lands believing that it weakened the authority of the king as well as reducing his future income, and immediate needs were met by two forced loans in 1622 and 1623. Forced loans were individual demands for money sent out to the wealthier members of society and were not usually repayable despite their name. Some of Cranfield's attempts to cut costs such as re-using a ten year old flag were despised by many at court who looked upon him as a mean and money-grubbing merchant.

As long as Cranfield had the support of James and Buckingham he could continue his campaign against waste. However, in 1623, Buckingham went to Madrid for six months (see page 46) and Cranfield took advantage of his absence to promote his nephew, Arthur Brett, as a new favourite. It was a risky gamble and it failed. James made Buckingham a duke to signal his continuing favour and when the duke returned he was eager for war against Spain. This would destroy any hope of reviving the king's finances and Cranfield opposed war strongly. As a result Charles and Buckingham used the Commons to impeach him for corruption. As James said 'All Treasurers if they do good service to their masters must be generally hated'. But James was not prepared to save his treasurer in the face of attacks by his favourite and his son. Cranfield had achieved some impressive savings and he had increased royal income by about £80,000. However, because he had tightened up the existing system rather than reforming it, he brought about no lasting improvement in crown finances. Ultimately, he left no permanent mark on royal solvency because the king could not restrain his extravagance. Even Cranfield, the would-be agent of reform, could not help feathering his own nest at royal expense so that he become one of the richest men in the country.

3 The Parliaments of 1621 and 1624

In 1621 James called a parliament. There had been no effective meeting of the nation's representatives since 1610 but it was not domestic concerns which led to their meeting. The worrying news from the Palatinate and the possibility of war prompted James to seek parliamentary finance. He wanted a speedy vote of supply and the Commons were anxious to be conciliatory, but mindful of the acute depression (which was to be the worst of the century) they felt able to grant only two subsidies (about £140,000) which was far short of what was required. Then they turned to domestic grievances and attention focused on monopolies. These had been an issue under Elizabeth and when he came to the throne James had announced his intention not to grant any patents of monopoly. No one objected to monopolies that were given to protect new inventions, but monopolies were also used to enable the crown to raise money by selling the exclusive right to provide a product (such as soap) or service (such as licensing ale-houses). Whatever the patentee paid, he would then recoup from the public because with the monopoly he could charge what he liked without fear of competition. As James's financial position had deteriorated he had increasingly issued patents of monopoly so that by 1621 there were over 100 and they had become a genuine grievance.

The Commons singled out Sir Giles Mompesson. In 1617 he had been granted a monopoly for the licensing of inns but instead of removing disorderly landlords he had granted a licence to anyone who would pay for it. The Commons sent charges up to the Lords against Mompesson who fled abroad. They stripped him of his knighthood and imposed a large fine on him. They moved on to examine other monopolies and James promised to revoke harmful patents. For once king and Commons were in harmony and a bill restricting monopolies failed only because of rejection by the Lords who might perhaps have lost by it.

Two privy councillors, Cranfield and the Lord Chief Justice Sir Edward Coke, took advantage of the Commons' attack on monopolies to rid themselves of a mutual rival. Sir Francis Bacon, the Lord

Chancellor, had approved a number of patents and could therefore be held responsible when they were abused. Coke, who was an expert in constitutional history and the common law, revived the ancient tool of impeachment last used in 1450 whereby the Commons acted as prosecutor and the Lords as judges. It was a dangerous weapon for royal officials to use as it could easily be turned against themselves, as Cranfield was to find in 1624. Bacon was accused of taking bribes, he pleaded guilty and was sentenced to a fine and imprisonment. James did not believe his Lord Chancellor had done anything worthy of dismissal but he was prepared to sacrifice him to appease the Commons and to prevent a possible attack on Buckingham, whose brothers had benefited from monopolies.

Up to this point all had gone well between king and Commons but then James proposed an adjournment. This reminded MPs of the failure of the Addled Parliament, which had been abruptly terminated, and made them apprehensive about a dissolution. Their fears were unfounded but the atmosphere of the House was completely different when it reassembled in November. There was little leadership from the crown and the Commons was left to set its own agenda. The most pressing problem was the Palatinate and the best means of securing it for Frederick. One of Buckingham's close associates made a speech which in effect invited the Commons to discuss foreign policy but matters soon got out of hand. They wanted to know who the enemy was and petitioned that Charles 'may be timely and happily married to one of our own religion'. James reacted angrily to this clear infringement of his prerogative which led to a series of sharp exchanges. He told the Commons not 'to meddle with anything concerning our government or deep matters of state' and that he felt 'very free and able to punish any man's misdemeanours in parliament, as well during their sitting as after it'.

The Commons replied 'Your Majesty doth seem to abridge us of the ancient liberty of Parliament for freedom of speech'. James then warned them 'that your privileges were derived from the grace and permission of our ancestors and us,' they should 'beware to trench upon the prerogative of the crown, which would enforce us, or any just king, to retrench them of their privileges'. The Commons then decided to enter a formal account of their privileges into their Journal in a document known as the Protestation. This put forward a strong defence of parliament and of free speech.

1 The liberties ... of parliament are the ancient and undoubted
   birthright [of the English] ... urgent affairs concerning the king,
   state and defence of the realm and of the Church of England and
   the maintenance and making of laws and redress of mischiefs and
5 grievances ... are proper subjects and matters of counsel and
   debate in parliament ... every member of the House of Parliament

hath, and of right ought to have, freedom of speech to propound, treat, reason, and bring to conclusion the same.

When he learnt about the Protestation, James sent for the Commons' Journal and ripped the page out. This was not a childish tantrum; he realised that if the Commons had the right to discuss foreign policy, they would in effect have a voice in the making of policy and the crown's freedom of action would be severely curtailed. The 1621 parliament was abruptly dissolved, it had passed a subsidy bill but no legislation and once again Crown and Commons had contrived to bring about a crisis. But now, with the added dynamite of religion and foreign affairs to make matters more explosive, the stakes were much higher and positions became more firmly entrenched.

Trouble had flared in the 1621 parliament when the Commons discussed foreign policy, yet in 1624 they were invited to do so again. This time conditions were very different. Charles and Buckingham had returned from Madrid bent on a war of revenge and their mood fitted the nation's. Only the reluctant James and some of the council stood in the way of war and parliament could be used to sweep objections aside. Charles regularly attended debates in the Upper House and was pleased at the anti-Spanish sentiment he found there. This made him ready to accept a number of potentially disturbing developments which made an old Scottish courtier comment 'it is very strange to see the Prince go on so in applauding all or the most part of the actions of a parliament which does every day grate upon the king's prerogative so much'. The three most important of these were the subsidy act, the statute of monopolies and the impeachment of Cranfield. The Commons approved the idea of a war but were less happy about the huge sums that would be needed, especially after bad harvests in both 1622 and 1623. To ensure a grant, Buckingham and Charles were prepared to accept restrictions upon the use to which the money could be put. In return for under £300,000, the crown agreed that the money would be used only for specific aspects of the war which were the defence of the realm, Ireland, aid to the United Provinces and the navy, and would be spent under the supervision of officials appointed by parliament. This did not indicate any great trust in the king and the idea of a continental expedition to the Palatinate was deliberately excluded. This was a dangerous precedent because it was a short step from specifying how money was to be spent to the formulation of policy. Parliament was unlikely to remain content for long with the former role.

The second attack on the king's prerogative was not intended as such but was a constitutional landmark as the first statutory limitation of the royal prerogative. The statue of monopolies was a restatement of the 1621 bill which had failed. The king's right to make grants to individuals was severely limited. No longer could patents of monopolies be issued except for new inventions, when they were limited to 14 years. However, the statute left a large loophole which was exploited by Charles's lord treasurers in the 1630s. Patents of monopoly could still be issued to chartered companies and corporations, so that anyone who wanted a monopoly had only to form themselves into a company and one could be issued legally. Thus, for example, in 1632 a very unpopular monopoly on soap manufacture was granted to a Catholic company of soap makers. The third action of the Commons which undermined royal authority but was encouraged by Charles and Buckingham was the impeachment of Cranfield. The Lord Treasurer was a strong supporter of Spain because he hoped that a Spanish dowry would cover most of the king's debts while he knew that war would undo all his attempts to improve the crown's financial position. The prince and the duke were determined to remove him but Cranfield still had the king's support. James knew that he was an efficient and reliable treasurer even if he made a large fortune for himself as well. Therefore, it was decided to use the parliamentary weapon of impeachment again. Cranfield was found guilty of corruption, he lost his offices, was fined £50,000, suffered imprisonment in the Tower and was barred from court. James who had felt unable to resist the demands of his son and favourite, nevertheless delivered a stern rebuke to each which was to be extraordinarily prophetic. Speaking of their intrigues with parliament he said to Buckingham:

1 You are a fool and will shortly repent this folly, and will find that in this fit of popularity you are making a rod with which you will be scourged yourself.
[Of Charles he said] ... he would live to have his bellyful of
5 parliaments, and that ... he would have too much cause to remember how much he had contributed to the weakening of the Crown by this precedent he was now so fond of ... as well the engaging the parliament in the war as the prosecution of the Earl of Middlesex [Cranfield].

The harmonious relations with the parliament of 1624 were full of potential danger for the crown. For the time being, the effective ruler (Charles) and the Commons were intent upon the same object, war with Spain. When their interests diverged, as was bound to happen, the Commons had been given some useful lessons in how to strengthen their position. They could restrict the way money was spent, unpopular ministers could be impeached, and disagreeable aspects of the king's prerogative could be curbed by legislation. It was not long before the Commons found it necessary to remember these lessons because almost immediately the crown swung away from its stated intentions. Charles and Buckingham had promised informally that there would be a war at sea. Instead there was no naval war nor even a breach with Spain, but against the express intentions of the Commons, Mansfeld's expedition (see page 49) was sent to the continent. Worse still, there were expensive undertakings to the Dutch and the Danes (see page 51). This was because James clung to the idea of peace with Spain to the end of his life and would only sanction a limited expedition to the continent. However, the effect was to create a distrust of Charles's word which would undermine his relations with parliament. To add insult to injury, Charles had promised parliament that no religious concessions would be made in the negotiations over a marriage treaty with France. This promise was broken when the recusancy laws were suspended and Henrietta Maria was allowed to worship freely in her own, public, chapel. Thus the position when James died in March 1625 was that the new king and his subjects were apparently united in a common purpose. In practice, royal actions had aroused deep suspicion about Charles's ultimate intentions, suspicion which would surface with unexpected rapidity.

4 The Parliament of 1625

Charles was eager for money to pursue the war against Spain and he was so confident of the reaction of parliament that he wanted to recall the parliament of 1624. When he was told that this had automatically been dissolved by James's death, he immediately issued writs for a new one. There was no attempt to woo MPs behind the scenes or to build up a government party and Charles seems to have believed that the new parliament would be as co-operative as the previous one. There was little guidance given in the direction of debates and, although Charles opened the session in June 1625 with an appeal for speedy supply and a promise to consider grievances later in the year, there was no indication given of the sum required. The Commons were anxious to demonstrate their loyalty to Charles and therefore voted two subsidies (about £140,000). This was totally inadequate and, against precedent, the Commons were asked for more. This gave an opportunity for the doubts to surface which had arisen since the 1624 parliament about the French marriage, Mansfeld's expedition and the lack of an enemy.

One prominent MP, Sir Robert Phelips, made an important speech which helped to sway the mood of the Commons away from the court. He declared that 'the promises and declarations of the last parliament were in respect of a war: we know yet of no war nor of any enemy'. However the king's preparations were real enough and against advice he continued to demand more supply. Plague was raging in London and MPs feared for their safety and wanted a quick adjournment, but first they had to vote tonnage and poundage. This customs revenue was traditionally granted to the king by the first parliament of his reign and provided a considerable portion of his income. It was supposed to be used to ensure the safety of shipping but in the 1620s privateers from North Africa were preying on ships and even raiding the coast which suggested that the money was being mis-applied. Only about one quarter of MPs were present and it was decided that a temporary grant of one year only would be made to give time for a full discussion of reform. The Commons were not only worried about the uses to which tonnage and poundage was put but also about impositions (customs duties). They wished to devise a new system which would give parliamentary sanction to the impositions which already existed but which would prevent the king granting any more. The Commons had good reasons for their actions and did not intend any personal slight to Charles but the king was deeply offended, especially as the Lords refused to pass the bill granting tonnage and poundage because they disliked innovation. Charles continued to collect tonnage and poundage without parliamentary sanction on a plea of necessity because he could not give up nearly half of his ordinary income when faced with a major war.

The plague grew worse and Charles adjourned the session in early July. But he ordered parliament to reassemble at Oxford three weeks later. This turned out to be a mistake. MPs who had already made clear their unwillingness to grant more money were not sympathetic to a demand for a speedy supply and turned their attention to Buckingham, whom they blamed for mishandling the session and the king's affairs. Charles regarded this attack as an attempt to undermine his authority and he dissolved parliament.

The first parliament of the reign had not been a success. Both king and Commons lost trust in each other. Charles felt betrayed. He did not understand how the Commons could fail to finance a war of which they had approved, and he bitterly resented the attacks on Buckingham and the failure to grant tonnage and poundage. He believed that the Commons were being led astray by a small group of conspirators who wished to undermine royal authority and that if they could be removed, harmony would be restored. The Commons were bewildered by the king's refusal to negotiate with them in the usual way. Charles was not prepared to trade the settling of grievances for the granting of money. He felt it was the Commons' duty to supply his needs first and then to trust him to attend to their problems. Throughout his reign, Charles displayed the utmost reluctance to bargain and already the Commons had found cause to doubt his word in the breaking of promises about the war and the marriage negotiations. Another worrying development for parliament was the favour shown to Arminians (see page 94). For the first time, the religion of the Crown was at variance with that of the majority of the representatives in parliament. This was to create great tension as the implications of the spread of Arminianism became clear in its effect on the doctrine and the worship of the Church of England.

5 The Parliament of 1626

The autumn of 1625 saw the failure of the expedition to Cadiz (see page

50). Undaunted, Charles and Buckingham pressed on with more military preparations. In a desperate search for funds, Charles had even secured a loan against the crown jewels. In February 1626 he summoned another parliament. In order to remove the malcontents whom he considered responsible for the failure of the last parliament Charles selected the most prominent as sheriffs for their counties. The sheriff was responsible for organising the polls and could not stand for election himself. By this means Charles removed Sir Robert Phelips, Sir Thomas Wentworth, Sir Edward Coke and Sir Francis Seymour from the Commons. However, his hope that this would transform the lower house was misplaced. It merely gave an opportunity for others to show their dissatisfaction.

Before parliament met, a conference of Puritans and Arminians was held at York House, one of Buckingham's homes. In this conference the favourite associated himself with the Arminians. In the Commons this increased the feelings against him which were already running high in the aftermath of the failure at Cadiz. Sir John Eliot, who had been a client of Buckingham's but who had turned against him in disgust at the mismanagement of the Cadiz expedition, took the lead. He demanded an enquiry into the expenditure of the 1624 subsidy and suggested that the crown's income could be increased by taking back excessive grants. This speech set the tone for the whole session which was described as 'a long discontent of eighteen weeks [which] brought forth nothing but a tympany of swelling faction and abrupt dissolution'.

The Commons wanted a scapegoat for the failures in foreign affairs and in their own relations with the king. They were in no doubt as to who was responsible. As one MP said:

> We must of necessity lay the fault upon somebody. Upon the king we cannot, seeing his care and great wisdom. And upon the Council we cannot. But on nobody but the Lord Admiral.

Alarmed at the direction of events, Charles summoned both Houses and warned them:

> Remember that parliaments are altogether in my power for their calling, sitting and dissolution. Therefore, as I find the fruits of them good or evil, they are to continue or not to be.

Undeterred by this threat, the Commons prepared articles of impeachment against Buckingham. Charles could not rely on the Lords dismissing the case against the duke and he decided to dissolve parliament. By doing so he abandoned the subsidies which had been promised but not enacted and left the war effort in a desperate financial predicament. Charles put his loyalty to his friend above good relations with his parliament and thereby soured the political atmosphere to the point where it would not give him the funds he needed to be successful at home or abroad.

In the aftermath of the parliament Buckingham reconciled himself to his most powerful opponent, the Earl of Pembroke, by arranging a marriage alliance between his own daughter and Pembroke's nephew and heir. Others opponents were swept out of office, including Lord Keeper Williams and Archbishop Abbot, who lost effective power although he remained Archbishop until his death in 1633. This narrowed the range of opinion represented on the Privy Council which increasingly followed the king's line and ceased to offer alternative advice after an open discussion. For example, it became difficult to talk about the rise of Arminianism or the calling of parliament.

6 The Forced Loan

The dissolution of parliament left the government with enormous outgoings on the war and no additional income other than captured French ships which brought in £50,000 in 1626. This was a mere drop in the ocean when the crown had undertakings of about one million pounds. In 1625, a forced loan worth two subsidies had been levied on Charles's richer subjects and in 1626 it was decided, against some opposition in the Council, to levy another forced loan worth five subsidies but this time on all subsidy payers. This was in effect parliamentary taxation that had not been sanctioned by parliament and there was considerable ill-feeling. As the Commons later told Charles 'there were never any monies demanded and paid with greater grief and general dislike of all your faithful subjects'. However, the method of collection discouraged most from refusing. By this method all subsidy payers were summoned to meetings where they were pressed individually to pay. In an unusually short time (by the end of 1627) over £260,000 had been raised which removed the threat of immediate bankruptcy from the crown. But this financial advantage had been brought at a heavy political cost.

A number of highly placed clerics who sought to further their careers rejected the idea that the king could only tax with consent. One said that tribute was 'due to princes ... by the law of god, as a sign of our subjection, by the law of nature, as the reward of their pains and protection' and 'by the law of nations as the sinews of the state's presentation'. This went directly against what many Englishmen had come to regard as a fundamental liberty - that they held sole rights in their own property and for the king to take it without consent was theft. If property was in danger then arbitrary government was being introduced and all other liberties were also at risk, not least the fate of parliament which would not be necessary if the king could tax his subjects when he wished as he was considered to be the sole judge of national necessity.

The loan itself was seen as attacking liberties. Charles's subsequent actions made fears about the imposition of absolutism much more acute. Seventy-six people, including prominent MPs such as Sir Thomas Wentworth, were imprisoned for refusing to pay the loan. When the judges would not pronounce that the loan was legal, Charles dismissed the Chief Justice of the King's Bench, Sir Ranulph Crewe. Five knights then challenged for habeas corpus (a fundamental right in English law whereby if due cause cannot be shown for imprisonment, a prisoner has to be released after 24 hours). It was too risky for the crown to allow the case (known as the Five Knights' Case) to come to court as the judges might release the knights, so the council stated that they had been imprisoned 'by special command of our lord the king'. So the king was not only taxing without consent but he was also imprisoning at his pleasure. Southern counties near where expeditions against France and Spain were being fitted out had the additional menace of billeting and martial law to contend with. Liberties of all kinds seemed to be under attack and the purging of religious dissidents in the universities and the introduction of religious practices that smacked of popery gave the king's intentions a more sinister aspect. Was his ultimate aim the extinction of all liberties and the establishment of a despotic Catholic regime?

Such an idea would doubtless have appeared absurd to Charles but he was too far removed from his subjects to appreciate what effect his actions had upon them. He believed that kings should be obeyed without question because their powers came from God. It was not necessary for the king to explain his actions: he merely needed to command. It followed that any opposition was illegitimate and the work of selfish or corrupt factions. Instead of worrying about unintended threats to liberty, Charles was much more concerned with obtaining sufficient money to prosecute the war effectively. The forced loan had helped in the short term but in September 1627 a treasury official warned Buckingham:

His Majesty's revenue of all kinds is now exhausted. We are upon the third year's anticipation beforehand; land, much sold of the principal; credit lost; and at the utmost shift with the commonwealth.

Charles had extracted another loan from the City but only by giving it the last major body of crown lands, worth 350,000 to cancel past debts and as security for the new loan. This ended the traditional role of land as a major source of royal revenue and meant the City was unwilling to lend in the future. Now the crown had to rely almost exclusively on the customs farmers but they could not supply all the king's needs. If Charles wanted more money he had only one option and that was to call parliament.

7 The Parliament of 1628-9

The parliament of 1626 had not been a happy precedent and both the king and the Commons realised they had reached a crisis point. If harmony was to be restored there would need to be gestures of reconciliation even though both sides felt they had justifiable grievances. The warnings were clear. One MP rousingly declared 'This is the crisis of parliaments. By this we shall know whether parliaments will live or die'. He went on to urge the Commons to be conciliatory to Charles 'by trusting the king, thereby to breed a trust in him towards us, for without a mutual confidence a good success is not to be expected'. Charles made his own position plain when he informed parliament that if it failed to provide funds to meet the common danger then 'I must, according to conscience, take those other courses which God hath put into my hands', which by implication excluded parliaments.

However, this option was not desired by anyone and the Council made efforts to create a good atmosphere. Buckingham reconciled himself to some political enemies such as the influential Earl of Arundel, no one was excluded from the Commons, and the loan prisoners were released. The Commons were also determined to make a success of the session. They quickly offered the king five subsidies which was unusually generous and agreed to grant him tonnage and poundage. But having demonstrated their loyalty they were concerned to safeguard the liberties of the subject. As one MP said 'we are told of dangers abroad but we have as great at home'.

a) The Petition of Right

The problem lay in how to proceed. It was obvious that the king would not accept any new law which defined the subject's rights (and therefore restricted the crown's freedom of action). It was held that Magna Carta and its accompanying legislation provided sufficient safeguards. To the Commons this was manifestly not the case as Charles's own actions in extracting the forced loan and imprisoning defaulters had shown. Sir Edward Coke suggested that the Commons and the Lords should present a joint petition to the king which, if he accepted it, would have the force of law. It is important to remember that the Commons did not believe they were acting in an innovatory manner. Their intention was to confirm what they regarded as being their traditional liberties. The conservatism of most of the Commons is seen in the fact that it was MPs or their social equivalents who had been responsible for collecting the forced loan. Although many considered the loan illegal, they did not question it in their role as leaders in the localities but waited to bring their dissent to parliament which was the correct place for its expression.

Charles did not accept this view of the role of parliament and he viewed the debates on the Petition of Right with deep disfavour. He wanted expressions of absolute trust and loyalty not restrictions on his freedom of action. He believed that the Commons had brought the forced loan upon themselves by their actions in refusing him money and that by the Petition of Right they were alienating his affections further. Charles wanted them to show 'that they rely on me and they shall find what they little expect'. In other words, he would be gracious and merciful. The problem was that the Commons did not trust him and they wanted some security for the future. Therefore they refused to accept a compromise from the Lords which left 'entire that sovereign power [the prerogative] wherewith Your Majesty is trusted'. The Lords then had to decide whether to join with the Commons in offering the Petition of Right or produce their own petition in which case neither would become law. Eventually they joined with the Commons. The Petition asked for an end to non-parliamentary taxation, imprisonment without cause, billeting, and martial law. The king accepted the Petition of Right but only with reluctance. His first reply did not use the traditional form of assent to bills which denied the Petition the force of law. The Commons insisted on the correct response and, as Charles was still waiting for them to pass the five subsidies they had agreed to, he gave the conventional assent.

The debates over the Petition of Right had shown deep alienation from the court. It was extraordinary that Charles could not rely on the House of Lords to protect his prerogative and that the Commons were reluctant to trust his word. Parliament was united in its belief that 'the Duke of Buckingham is the cause of all our miseries' and the Commons drew up a remonstrance identifying the threats which faced them from innovations in religion, including lax enforcement of the laws against Catholics, innovation in government and disasters and dangers at home and abroad. The failures of Buckingham's foreign policy could easily be seen as the judgement of God upon a government that had turned away from the true light of Protestantism towards the false lure of Rome. When the Commons began work on a second remonstrance which denounced the unparliamentary collection of tonnage and poundage as contrary to the Petition of Right, Charles prorogued parliament in June. He had obtained the five subsidies but not confirmation of the customs. He continued to collect tonnage and poundage out of necessity. When this was challenged by merchants who refused to pay, the courts supported the king and said that the Petition of Right was too general to be used against its collection. It seemed that the Commons were right to distrust the king.

b) The Death of Buckingham

In August 1628 Buckingham was assassinated (see page 54), to the intense joy of the nation and sorrow of the king. The scenes of public rejoicing at his friend's death seem to have scarred Charles and to have played a part in distancing him from his people. He blamed parliament for Buckingham's death because Felton said he had been inspired by the remonstrance which named Buckingham as the cause of the nation's ills. There were only 100 mourners at Buckingham's funeral and the coffin was empty because the duke had been secretly buried the night before in case hostile crowds tried to attack his body. As one man wrote:

Here lies the best and worst of fate,
Two kings' delight, the people's hate.

The death of Buckingham was a turning point in the reign. Henceforth Charles withdrew much more into himself and there was no longer an obvious target for those who disliked royal policies. Slowly it came to be realised that Charles himself, rather than evil counsellors, was responsible. The death of Buckingham and the end of his ruinous foreign policy might have been expected to produce better relations between king and Commons when parliament reassembled in January 1629. It was not to be.

c) The End of the Parliament of 1628-9

The second session was dominated by two issues: Arminianism and tonnage and poundage. Charles had made a number of concessions over religion. The recusancy laws were enforced again and Archbishop Abbot was readmitted to the Privy Council, but this was not enough to quell the fears of many in the Commons. Arminians had been steadily increasing in influence. Richard Montagu became Bishop of Chichester and Laud moved from Bath to London, the most important position in the Church after Canterbury, which enabled him, with the king's support, to undermine the position of Archbishop Abbot. The Commons resolved unanimously that religion should take precedence over all business and they wanted to bargain with the customs to obtain religious concessions. Charles was not prepared to weaken his support for the Arminians and the session was therefore doomed.

Other matters also troubled the Commons. The first was that the printed version of the Petition of Right contained Charles's initial, unsatisfactory answer which had the effect of weakening the Petition's impact. It was a highly dubious act by Charles and contributed to the growth of distrust in the king's sense of honour. The second matter for concern was the seizure of goods from merchants who had refused to pay tonnage and poundage, one of whom was an MP. It became obvious that the Commons were not going to make Charles a grant of the customs which was his main reason for holding a second session. He decided on an adjournment but when the speaker informed the Commons of this and attempted to rise from his chair to end the session, he was forcibly held down by two MPs while Sir John Eliot called out three resolutions. These condemned as 'a capital enemy to the king and commonwealth' anyone who promoted innovation in religion, popery or Arminianism; anyone who counselled the collection of tonnage and poundage without parliamentary consent; and anyone who voluntarily paid the duties. The three resolutions are interesting for the link they made between arbitrary government and Arminianism and the notion that innovation was something to be condemned.

The resolutions were passed with shouts of acclamation and then the House voted to adjourn itself. It was an extraordinary scene with Black Rod hammering on the door for admittance and the speaker struggling to free himself. It came as no surprise to anyone that Charles then dissolved parliament and imprisoned those involved in the demonstration. Their appeals for freedom based on the Petition of Right were ignored, showing that the Petition had little effect in safeguarding liberties when the king chose to ignore it. Charles's third parliament, like its two predecessors had come to an unhappy end. He resolved to do without them in future.

Buckingham's death did not solve all the conflicts between Charles and parliament as many contemporaries had undoubtedly hoped it would. The assassination of the Duke removed the main impetus to an expensive policy of warfare which had long ceased to be popular, but in domestic affairs the guiding hand behind the creation of policy was revealed to be that of the king. In four years, the initial approval of Charles had been transformed into serious misgivings about his intentions in religion and whether he would respect the liberties of his subjects. Suspicion led to a lack of co-operation from parliament and Charles was understandably frustrated in his attempt to rule in accordance with tradition when the Commons would not grant him the revenues that traditionally were due to him.

8 Assessment of James as King of Scotland and England

If James had died in 1603 he would be remembered as an effective and skilful ruler of Scotland. For at least two hundred years the Scottish nobility had enjoyed extensive powers which had been gained at the expense of the crown. This problem had greatly increased in the sixteenth century, especially during the long period (1542-83) when Scotland had been without strong royal leadership. The great magnates had come to regard it as their right to control the government and they engaged in conspiracies to further their aims. By 1600 James had survived five plots by different aristocratic factions to take control of the state by seizing his person. These experiences had strengthened his hatred of violence and had increased his belief in the divine nature of royal authority and in the evils of revolt whatever the circumstances. They also enabled him to reduce the power of the nobility so that there was no trouble in Scotland after 1603 despite the absence of the king. James learned how to balance sections of the nobility against each other.

He continued the practice of making landlords responsible for the behaviour of their tenants and by judicious use of rewards he fostered a sense of loyalty to himself.

The mid-century, when crown fortunes were at their lowest, had seen the adoption of the Reformation. The Calvinist Church which resulted had been supported by important sections of the nobility. The alliance of clergy and nobles could be a potent and dangerous force. The Church in Scotland was a tightly-knit body which exercised great power. If it united with the nobility against the king, he could do little against them. One of James's greatest triumphs was to break this alliance. This enabled him to introduce bishops in 1618, and meant that he could leave Scotland in 1603, secure in the knowledge that the nobles had been tamed and that the Church could do little without their support. James returned to Scotland only once. This was in 1617, when he tactlessly lectured his fellow countrymen on the superiority of English civilisation.

This was a typical example of James acting in an ill-considered way and it was to be repeated frequently once he was King of England. He seems to have had little or no appreciation of the effect his speeches would have. In view of his earlier life, it was perfectly reasonable of James to be wary of anything that seemed to indicate undue pressure and this was why he disliked petitioners approaching him. But it was a mistake to assume that anyone who opposed him was either seriously challenging his authority or was on the verge of revolt. Many of James's problems with his parliaments could have been solved with more diplomatic handling. The Commons were not blameless because they were far too ready to identify an attack upon their privileges when often none was intended, but the king often turned an incident into a crisis by stating that all parliament's privileges derived from him and, by implication, could therefore be taken away, when in reality he had no intention of undermining parliament's position.

The crucial quality of kingship which James lacked was leadership. More than anything else this was symbolised by James's habit of leaving the centre of affairs to go hunting. Half his reign was spent out of London while the Privy Council tried to keep the government running smoothly, often in the absence of specific instructions because James was incurably lazy. Sessions of parliament suffered from this lack of direction. In the absence of an agenda from the court, the Commons would set their own and they usually discussed financial grievances - purveyance in 1604 and impositions in 1614. James had been used to a more informal system in Scotland where he could sit in parliament and vote. In such circumstances it was easier to direct debates and ensure that government business was pushed through. In England, if James wanted to say anything to the Commons, he had either to speak through his privy councillors who were members of the House or to summon both Houses to a formal audience when he could address them. This latter was a cumbersome means of making royal wishes known but because there had been no effort made to ensure adequate representation for privy councillors (there were only two in the first parliament, both mediocre speakers), it was sometimes necessary. This had the unfortunate side-effect that it enabled James to indulge his passion for listening to the sound of his own voice at great length:

> Upon Wednesday last [March 1610] both of the Houses being assembled in the Banqueting-House at Whitehall, his Majesty made them a speech of two hours long; wherein he showed great learning, admirable memory, and exceeding piety...

James was tactless, pedantic, undignified and lazy but all of this would

James I of England and VI of Scotland by Daniel Mytens, 1621

have been forgotten or at least forgiven if it had not been for his appalling extravagance and liberality to all those around him. His favourites aroused moral disapproval but it was the gifts which were lavished upon them which really upset the country. At a time when the crown itself was in financial difficulty, it was foolish at best for James to pay the debts of some of his more spendthrift courtiers as he did in 1607 to the tune of £44,000. Lord Hay, one of the recipients, used to joke 'Spend and God will send' an assessment which was all too accurate under James.

This level of expenditure put great strain on the traditional means of financing the government as increasingly the country was asked to supplement royal revenue with parliamentary grants. Taxes would never be popular, but when they were requested so that more gifts could be given to the hateful Scots there was bound to be serious trouble. So parliament and James who might well have worked in harmony if money had not been a constant issue, came to regard the intentions of the other with suspicion and distrust. The financial system proved incapable either of restraining the extravagance of the king or of providing the funds to satisfy him. The result was the worst of both worlds, James continued to spend as freely as he wanted making occasional promises to stop, while the crown staggered from one financial crisis to the next, raising money wherever it could be found- from customs farmers, the sale of titles or outright corruption. In the process its dignity suffered great damage and the rhetorical speeches of James emphasising the divine nature of kingly power merely served to show how far from the ideal reality had moved. Men were not yet disillusioned with the crown but the questioning and criticism of royal actions was becoming a well-established part of parliamentary proceedings.

James was a king with many good qualities which tended to be obscured by a few glaring faults. Historians are divided on whether the good outweighed the bad or whether James deserves more criticism than praise.

Making notes on 'Domestic Politics, 1618-29'

This chapter covers a crucial part of the period, when relations between the crown and parliament reached the point where they could no longer work constructively together. There are a number of questions to be borne in mind as you make notes on the chapter.

- What went wrong?
- Was it crown policies or the obstructiveness of parliament?
- How great a role did personality play in the growth of distrust?
- Was there a difference between James and Charles?
- What effect did the Duke of Buckingham have on the history of these years?
- How serious was the rift between Charles I and parliament by 1629?

Historians writing about this period will often lay the blame on either the crown or the Commons, or Buckingham will appear as the arch-villain. There were faults on all sides and this is an area where you can draw your own conclusions and support them convincingly with evidence from what happened.

The following headings and questions are suggested as a framework for your notes.

1   The Duke of Buckingham
     Buckingham's rise and the extent of his power
1.1 Effect on the system of government
1.2 Reasons for Buckingham's unpopularity
2   Cranfield and the King's Finances
     Cranfield's background. The state of royal finances
2.1 The Campaign against Waste
     Were the economies merely superficial? Did he bring about any structural reform of crown finances?
2.2 Assessment of Cranfield as Lord Treasurer
     Why was he unable to achieve more? What brought his downfall?
3   The Parliament of 1621
     Why was it called? Monopolies. The Protestation.
3.1 The Parliament of 1624
     Explain how the balance between crown and parliament was altered
3.2 The Subsidy
3.3 The Statute of Monopolies
3.4 The Impeachment of Cranfield
4   The Parliament of 1625
     Explain why this first parliament of the new reign was a failure
5   The Parliament of 1626
6   The Forced Loan
7   The Parliament of 1628-9
7.1 The Petition of Right
     What was the Petition? Why was it important?
7.2 The Assassination of Buckingham
7.3 The End of the Parliament
8   Assessment of James as King
8.1 In Scotland
8.2 In England
     Using two columns, write down James's qualities. Put good qualities in one column and bad ones in the other. Then write down your judgement of the king.

Answering essay questions on 'Domestic Politics, 1618-29'

This chapter spans parts of two reigns. Examiners do set questions in which the dates do not correspond to those of the ruler but it is much more common for them to ask about one king at a time. For this reason the following questions will concentrate on James's reign. To answer them you will need to refer back to chapter 3 as well. Study these questions.

1   'It was not his policies but the way he tried to carry them out that led James I into so many conflicts with his parliaments'. Discuss.
2   Do you agree that James I lacked the personal qualities necessary to be a successful ruler of England in the early seventeenth century?
3   What mistakes were made by James I in his first ten years as King of England which prejudiced his relations with his English subjects?
4   'Relations between crown and parliament deteriorated seriously in the reign of James I'. How far would you agree with this view?
5   Were James I's problems of his own making?
6   Why was finance the most persistent of the causes of tension between James I and his parliaments?
7   Have James I's abilities as King of England been underrated?
8   Assess and account for the influence of George Villiers, Duke of Buckingham.
9   Compare the careers of Lionel Cranfield, Earl of Middlesex and George Villiers, Duke of Buckingham.

You will see that all the questions except the last two are about James and they all require you to produce an opinion rather than a staightforward account of events. These can seem rather daunting, especially early on in your course, but they have one major advantage. It is much easier to see two sides to this sort of question and this will help in constructing an argument. You may have strong opinions about some of the questions but you must explain why an opposing point of view is not convincing, which involves explaining what that point of view is. Then use the conclusion to put the case for your own ideas - as forcefully as you like! Notice the assumption being made in most of the questions about who was responsible for the problems.

The last two questions are about Buckingham. It is important not to fall into the trap of mere description which would be easy in question 9. For this question take key points from their careers and compare them throughout the essay. Do not look at Cranfield and then Buckingham in separate sections, only comparing them in your conclusion. It is more effective - and more impressive- if you can weave your comparisons into the body of the essay. You might like to use the following headings as a basis for the essay:

- rise to power
- official positions held
- main sphere of operations
- scope of influence
- reaction of others
- downfall.

Source-based questions on 'Domestic Politics, 1618-29'

1 The Duke of Buckingham
Carefully read the list of Buckingham's offices printed on page 62. Then look closely at Buckingham's portrait on page 63 and answer the following questions.
a)   Look carefully at the list of Buckingham's titles and offices. Did they in themselves justify the charge that 'all the king's Council ride upon one horse'? (5 marks)
b)   What words would best describe Buckingham as he appears in his portrait? Think carefully about how he has chosen to dress. (2 marks)
c)   Why was it necessary for him to appear in this way? (3 marks)

2 The Protestation
Carefully read the exchanges between James and the Commons in the 1621 parliament given on pages 68-9. Answer the following questions.
a)   Why was freedom of speech considered so essential by the House of Commons? (5 marks)
b)   How would you describe James's attitude to the Commons? (3 marks)
c)   What rights were the Commons claiming in the Protestation? (7 marks)
d)   In your opinion was the king or the Commons more justified in their stand over the Protestation? (5 marks)

3 James's Warning to Charles and Buckingham
Carefully read the warning given by James to Charles and Buckingham on page 70 and the exchanges between Charles and the Commons on page 73. Answer the following questions.
a)   What was James referring to when he warned Buckingham of 'a rod with which you will be scourged yourself'? (2 marks)
b)   How far was James proved right in his warning to Charles by events in 1625-6? (5 marks)
c)   Describe the change in Charles's attitude to parliament between James's warning to him in 1624 and his address to the Commons in

1626. (3 marks)
d) How does the comment by the MP account for this change?
(2 marks)

4 The Portrait of James I

Study carefully the portrait of James I painted by Daniel Mytens in 1621, given on page 81. Answer the following questions.
a) What adjectives would you use to describe James? (4 marks)
b) What indications are there that James is a king? (3 marks)
c) Compare this portrait with the one of Charles I on page 115. What significant detail is missing from the picture of James which you might have expected to find? (2 marks)
d) Does this portrait fit in with your impression of James? Give reasons for your answer. (6 marks)

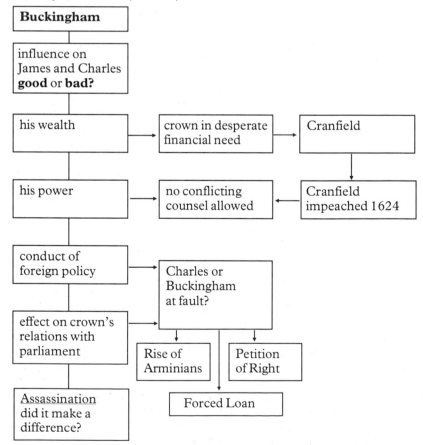

Summary - Domestic Politics, 1618-29

CHAPTER 6

Religion, 1603-40

1 The Position in 1603

In the early modern period, religion played a crucial role in almost everybody's life. There was little toleration in the realm of religion. There was truth and there was error and the two were not be confused by an over-charitable attitude to those who had different beliefs. These beliefs mattered because they determined whether an individual's soul went to heaven or hell. In the seventeenth century religious beliefs were thought to be literally a question of life and death on an eternal timescale. This is why enormous passions were aroused over such apparently trivial matters as the use of a ring in marriage which was objected to by the Puritans because such symbols indicated a residual belief in the (as they saw it) idolatry of Catholicism.

The Church of England had been established by a number of acts of parliament at the start of Elizabeth I's reign after the upheavals of the mid-sixteenth century under Edward and Mary. Elizabeth had been anxious to secure her position and not to drive people into opposition. As a result, the church settlement contained elements of deliberate ambiguity. For example, the services were Protestant but could have a Catholic meaning imparted to them if people wanted them to. This worked admirably in the short term and within thirty years the vast majority of the population had been won over to the new Church. However, there remained a hard core of Catholics who refused to attend their parish church and thus were liable to large fines as recusants, and a Protestant minority which felt that the Elizabethan reforms did not go far enough. They wished to purify the Church of all remaining taint of Roman Catholic practice. They were known as Puritans. They ranged from a few extremists (separatists) who wished to separate from the Church of England to form an independent church, to a much larger number who detested and distrusted anything to do with Catholicism but who would have been content with only minor modifications to the Church of England. It was these two groups - Catholics and Puritans - who awaited the arrival of James I in 1603 with the greatest hopes and fears.

The Reformation in Scotland had taken a very different course to the one in England. In the early 1560s John Knox, a fiery preacher who had been trained in Geneva, led the Scottish Church in a Calvinist reformation that overthrew the bishops and established a Presbyterian form of church government. James was brought up in this rigid and unyieldingly Protestant atmosphere. Therefore, the Puritans could reasonably hope that their new king would be more sympathetic to their demands than Elizabeth had been. However, the Catholics also had reason to expect better things because of James's known toleration of beliefs which differed from his own and because his wife (Anne of Denmark) had converted to Catholicism.

2 James I and the Catholics

Catholic persecution in England had become more severe after the outbreak of war with Spain in the 1580s. Catholics were seen as potential traitors, which a handful had confirmed by their involvement in plots revolving around Mary, Queen of Scots. Fines for recusants were increased and 146 Catholics were executed between 1586 and 1603, either for being or for sheltering priests. James promised that he would not 'persecute any that will be quiet and give an outward obedience to the law'. The Catholics hoped that they would be able to practise their faith in private unmolested by the law and its recusancy fines. At this time attendance at the local parish church was compulsory and persistent non-attendance would result in the imposition of fines. These could be crippling and if the Catholic gentry were not to be ruined they needed a relaxation of the law.

At first the Catholics were not disappointed. James ordered the recusancy fines to be reduced and they fell to less than a quarter of their level before 1603. But this leniency was to be short-lived. In 1604 all priests and Jesuits were ordered out of the kingdom and in November recusancy fines were ordered to be collected in full. The reason for this abrupt change of policy was almost certainly the adverse reaction toleration provoked amongst James's Protestant subjects. The 1604 parliament passed an act calling for 'due execution of the statutes' against 'any manner of recusants'. The king did not want to antagonise parliament when he was trying to promote his cherished dream of union between England and Scotland. Therefore, he was ready to use the Catholics as a bargaining counter. He hoped that if he agreed to the request for harsher measures against Catholics, parliament would make concessions over the terms of union.

The blow to the Catholic community was severe and encouraged a few to seek a more extreme remedy for their troubles. Peace with Spain in 1604 had deprived the Catholics of the hope of foreign intervention to promote their cause. In desperation, a plot was hatched to remove the king and his entire government at a stroke. This, of course, was the Gunpowder Plot whose failure is still commemorated every November 5th.

a) The Gunpowder Plot (1605) and its Consequences

Some years ago it was suggested that the Gunpowder Plot was an invention of Robert Cecil to give him an excuse to attack the Catholics. There is something appealing about the notion of one of our most enduring national celebrations being founded on a myth, but in fact there is little doubt that there really was a plot. The conspiracy centred on the digging of a tunnel under the Houses of Parliament which would then be blown up when James was attending the opening of a new session. The main plotters came from gentry families which probably suffered most from recusancy fines. The plot was revealed when one conspirator sent a warning to a relative to keep away from parliament.

James was upset by the plot. The Venetian ambassador reported that 'the king is in terror. He does not appear nor does he take his meals in public as usual. He lives in the innermost rooms with only Scotsmen about him'. Recusancy fines were increased and Catholics were forbidden to live in or near London or to hold public office. They were also required to take a new oath of allegiance which denied the Pope's authority to depose kings. The Pope opposed the oath but most Catholics were happy to demonstrate their political loyalty by taking it.

The Catholics gave James no further trouble. The were allowed to practise their religion albeit at a financial cost. The penal laws (imposing fines) were often ordered to be enforced more strictly when a parliament was due to meet as a concession to the violently anti-Catholic Commons. However, Catholicism did not become a major political issue until after the outbreak of the Thirty Years War in 1618. Then a number of events combined to increase fears about popery and the crown's commitment to true religion. James's attempts to secure a Spanish bride for Charles, the failure to support the Protestant cause on the continent, and the relaxation of the recusancy laws in 1622-3 as part of the negotiations with Spain all contributed to a growth in anti-Catholicism which would increase as fears about the advance of popery at home and abroad intensified.

3 James I and the Puritans

Despite his Presbyterian upbringing, James was not temperamentally attached to the Scottish Kirk. This may owe something to the behaviour of Scottish churchmen such as Andrew Melville who, in 1596, shook James's sleeve and called him 'God's silly vassal'. James preferred the more ordered worship of the Church of England and its hierarchical government by bishops. His instinctive reaction to the demands of the Millenary Petition supposedly signed by 1000 clergy, which asked for moderate Puritan reforms and was handed to him as he travelled south in 1603, was to regard it with suspicion as the thin end of a wedge which might ultimately lead to a Presbyterian system. This was a mistake, the vast majority of English Puritans wanted moderate, piecemeal reforms to cleanse the Church of the last vestiges of Popish practice.

James announced that he would hold a conference at Hampton Court in January 1604 at which bishops and Puritans could debate the issues raised by the Millenary Petition. The conference would consider the demand for an end to what were seen as popish ceremonies and would also look at wider Church issues. These included pluralism and the endowment of a preaching ministry. There was a general desire to see the quality of the clergy improved. Because stipends were so low, many clergymen were forced to hold more than one living just to survive, but this left many parishes with inadequate pastoral care. It was therefore necessary to find some means of increasing the payment of the clergy if pluralism was to be eradicated. The demand for a preaching ministry showed the importance which Puritans placed on the teaching of the Word (the Bible). This was designed to dispel ignorance and encourage individual concern over spiritual development. It was not only Puritans who were concerned about the state of the Church. Many with different beliefs also wished to see standards raised. James himself took a close interest in religious affairs and was genuinely interested in reform. Much might therefore have been expected of the conference, but it failed to live up to its promise.

a) The Hampton Court Conference, 1604

The conference was a disputation (formal debate) between several bishops and four or five Puritans chosen by the Privy Council. These were moderate men and the radical Puritans were disappointed not be represented. In general the discussions were harmonious and there was much general agreement. A new version of the Bible was decided upon which appeared in 1611 as the Authorised or King James Bible. However, the conference was a failure for the Puritans because they failed to win any of their demands. There were a number of reasons for this.

First, if they suggested any major alteration of Church government, such as the removal of bishops, they would be branded as extremists and nothing would be achieved. The Puritans therefore pursued the opposite line. Their demands, such as not having to wear a surplice, were so moderate that James dismissed their grievances as trivial and unworthy of note.

Secondly, the Puritans wished to impress the king with the strength of their following and a petitioning campaign was organised in many areas of the country. This backfired because James disliked being subjected to what he saw as undue pressure and it also revealed an alarming degree of lay and clerical organisation. The last thing James wanted was a Presbyterian church on the Scottish model in which ministers asserted that he was subject to church discipline like any other member. Accordingly when the word Presbytery was mentioned, James burst out with 'No bishop, no king', although this did not bring the conference to an end.

The Puritans were not granted any changes in church organisation or practice. And although there was agreement between them and the bishops on two other matters, parliament failed to take the necessary steps to make the reforms effective. The first of these was the attempt to end the excessive use of excommunication as a punishment for contempt of court. Excommunication (which prevented an individual from taking part in church services and therefore put his immortal soul in danger of going to hell) was a powerful weapon of the church courts. Its use in secular courts undermined church discipline. However, parliament did not enact the legislation that would have been needed to outlaw the use of excommunication in the common law courts.

The second area of agreement was that action was needed on the poverty of the Church. Since the dissolution of the monasteries in the mid-sixteenth century, vast amounts of church lands had passed into lay hands and, more significantly, so had the tithes from many parishes leaving insufficient to support a minister. Archbishop Whitgift had estimated in the 1580s that only 600 out of 9000 parishes provided an adequate stipend. Parliament made sympathetic noises about the poverty of the Church but ultimately was unwilling to act because its members were often the ones who benefited from impropriation of tithes and they considered any reform as an attack upon their property rights.

The Hampton Court Conference brought little consolation to those Puritans who had looked to James for reform. Their demands had been dismissed as trivial or had failed because of the vested interests of those in parliament. Worse, James himself now regarded the Puritans with some suspicion. On the death of Archbishop Whitgift he appointed Richard Bancroft, who was determined to enforce the uniformity of the Church, as his successor.

b) The Enforcement of Conformity

In February 1604 James ordered Convocation (the Church equivalent of a parliament) to draw up a new book of Canons (church laws) which would resolve disputed matters. The most important of these Canons required all ministers to subscribe to three articles supporting the king's supremacy, agreeing to the 39 Articles (the doctrines of the Church of England), and accepting 'that the Book of Common Prayer ... containeth nothing in it contrary to the Word of God'. They also had to promise to use only the authorised services. This was an attack on Puritan lecturers who, on Sunday afternoons, were accustomed to give long sermons with no formal service. These articles were a serious blow to many Puritans because they could no longer try to ignore practices of which they disapproved. They now had to affirm their support for them. About 90 Puritan ministers could not bring themselves to conform and so lost their livings. A much larger number remained within the Church, protected by a friendly bishop or merely accepting the inevitable.

The strict enforcement of uniformity did not last long. When Bancroft died in 1610 the new Archbishop was George Abbott, a Calvinist who was sympathetic to the Puritans. There was a general desire to see a more learned ministry and many bishops sought to encourage this by preaching frequently themselves. This was welcomed by those who leant towards Puritanism and in towns across the country lectureships were endowed which neighbouring clergy and the townspeople were encouraged to attend. Non-conformity over such matters as not wearing the surplice or signing with the cross in baptism gradually reappeared and was generally tolerated by the authorities. Until 1618 religious divisions within the Church seemed to have been resolved and a wide variety of practices were accepted.

4 Religious Divisions Reappear, 1618-25

The outbreak of the Thirty Years War increased religious polarisation and brought many tensions to the surface. Up to 1629 the Catholic armies of the Emperor and the Spanish swept all before them. The very existence of Protestantism in Germany seemed to be under threat. Fears about the international spread of Catholicism were heightened by the Spanish marriage negotiations which, if successful, would mean a Catholic queen and Catholic worship in London. An apparent change in James's attitude to religion increased the worries of many.

James had always been Calvinist in his theology even if he disliked the Calvinist method of church organisation. This meant he believed in predestination which was the standard orthodoxy of the Church of England. A Dutch theologian - Jacob Arminius - attacked Calvin's doctrine of predestination and asserted that men had free will to decide their own fate, because God willed the salvation of all who believed. The followers of Arminius were known as Arminians. Apart from free will, they believed in services which were more ceremonial and put more stress on the sacraments. They regarded the Catholic church as being in error but still a true church, and they tended to exalt the power of the Crown.

James was at first an opponent of Arminius and sent representatives to argue against him in 1618. However, towards the end of his reign he became more sympathetic to the Arminian cause because of the practical support it gave him. The 1620s saw mounting protests against Spain and Catholicism and questions about the Crown's handling of foreign policy. The Arminians upheld royal authority and did not share the irrational hatred of popery. It was natural, therefore, for James to promote Arminians, a development that was regarded with suspicion by many in the Commons who regarded Arminians as little better than papists.

In 1622 James issued instructions to the clergy forbidding 'popular' preaching about predestination or 'reprobation' (damnation). This may have been partly because preachers were using sermons to criticise the king's foreign policy, or it may reflect a genuine change of heart by James. In 1624 he allowed the publication of an Arminian book by

Richard Montagu. It is interesting to speculate whether, if James had survived throughout the 1620s, he would have encountered the same problems as Charles, with king and Commons frequently clashing over religion. It is probable that he would not have because he was more in tune with the religious beliefs of the country and was ready to listen to opposing views. His commitment to the Protestant cause was not in doubt. Charles was very different. He promoted the apparently semi-Catholic Arminianism without thought of the consequences and the opposition it would provoke in parliament. He believed that he was right and that his policies should be accepted without question. This meant that actions by James would be tolerated, whereas similar decisions caused an outcry under Charles. This was demonstrated by the Book of Sports, which listed the activities considered lawful on Sundays after church. These included dancing and archery but not bull- or bear-baiting. The book was originally issued by James in 1618 after an attempt by magistrates in Lancashire to suppress such activities. Anything which smacked of frivolity was distasteful to Puritans on the sabbath. James ordered the book to be read from the pulpit. This offended many clergy who felt that by so doing they appeared to agree with its contents. However, the Book raised relatively few protests. After another Puritan attack on Sunday activities, Charles reissued the Book of Sports in 1633. This time there was much greater opposition because it seemed to be part of a wider strategy to undermine the traditional Church of England.

5 Religion in Scotland and Ireland, 1603-25

As Conrad Russell has pointed out, James and Charles were unique among European rulers in having multiple kingdoms divided over religion and 'in all of which there existed a powerful group which preferred the religion of one of the others to their own'. In an age which believed that religious differences led to political dissent, it was natural for the ruler to seek uniformity throughout his territories. In 1607 the two Earls of Ulster fled into exile following the failure of an earlier rebellion. Their lands were confiscated and given to Calvinist Scots and English settlers in what is known as the plantation of Ulster. This meant that there were three faiths in Ireland: the Catholic majority, the established Church of Ireland which was much more uniformly Calvinist than its English counterpart, and a smaller group of newly arrived Presbyterians. In this situation the enforcement of religious uniformity would be a difficult and potentially dangerous task. It was one that James, wisely, did not undertake.

   In Scotland the position was less complicated. James's ultimate aim was to bring the Scottish Church into conformity with the Church of England. He must have known that there could not be complete harmonisation but he was determined to introduce bishops. He succeeded in winning the nobles away from their former alliance with the Kirk. It was this alliance that had pushed through the Reformation in Scotland and without the nobles' support the Kirk was much less able to resist royal demands. Bishops were therefore imposed in 1618, although the underlying Presbyterian structure remained, and James forced a number of liturgical reforms through the general (church) assembly. These 'Articles of Perth' were deeply unpopular, especially the one that prescribed kneeling to receive communion, and James realised he had gone too far. The Articles were not strictly enforced and a new prayer book which had been prepared in 1619 was not introduced. In this way James avoided open religious conflict, a sensitivity which Charles was not to share.

6 The Rise of Arminianism, 1625-30

A change in religious tone was evident within a few weeks of Charles I's accession. One Arminian (William Laud) was chosen to preach the opening sermon of the first parliament of the reign. Another (Richard Montagu) became a royal chaplain and later Bishop of Chichester. After Laud became Bishop of London in 1628, second in influence within the Church to the Archbishop of Canterbury, all leading church posts were filled by Arminians and Calvinists were progressively excluded from the king's counsels. An early indication of the new climate was seen at Cambridge University where all teaching on predestination was forbidden after Buckingham's installation as chancellor in 1626.

How should one view the growth of Arminianism? In the 1970s Nicholas Tyacke produced a crucial new interpretation of the religious history of Charles's reign which reversed the previous historical orthodoxy. Instead of the Puritans being seen as the innovators who undermined the Church of England, Tyacke suggests that Charles and Laud were the reformers. The king and his Arminian bishops attempted to alter the traditional beliefs and practices of the Church and branded the majority of English people who disagreed with their reforms as Puritans. In this analysis, the Puritans were the opposite of radical. Far from wishing to change the belief of the Church of England, they clung to the long-established Calvinist doctrines of damnation and salvation in the face of an attack by the Arminians. Tyacke's thesis has been widely accepted, although inevitably there are some dissenting voices, notably Kevin Sharpe in a major study of the personal rule published in 1992. What did it mean to be an Arminian under Charles and what was the king trying to achieve through his policies?

a) Arminianism

As with many labels the term 'Arminian' is used to cover a considerable variety of practice and belief. Not all Arminians accepted the doctrine of free will but they were united by a concern over church ceremonial and worship. One feature of the Arminians was that they wished to worship 'in the beauty of holiness' in buildings which were dedicated only to sacred use and where services were conducted in a reverent and dignified manner. There was much in the existing Church of England to cause them distress - many churches were in a serious state of disrepair, while in others animals were allowed to wander freely. A wide variety of practice had grown up in the conduct of services. At one extreme there might be no decoration or music, the communion table would be in the centre of the church, and the service would revolve around the sermon. At the other extreme there would be elaborate ritual, the altar railed in at the east end of the church, bowing at the name of Jesus, a short homily rather than a sermon, and great stress laid upon the sacraments, especially the eucharist (the service of communion).

Arminians tended not to enquire too deeply into men's beliefs but did insist upon uniformity of worship in accordance with the prescribed liturgy of the Church of England. They wanted this uniformity to be maintained through the authority of the bishops and clergy. Individuals who promoted or supported greater piety through such activities as lectures were regarded with suspicion as a possible threat to order and the established hierarchy. Because of their stress on obedience to authority, Arminians tended to exalt the royal prerogative, as when Robert Sibthorpe preached in favour of the forced loan in 1627. The appeal of Arminianism to Charles was clear - it mirrored his own concern with order, obedience and hierarchy. Personally and politically, Arminianism fulfilled his needs.

b) Clashes with Parliament, 1625-9

Arminianism suited Charles but the House of Commons viewed it in a very different light. Religion, which had not been a political issue under James I, suddenly became an additional point of conflict between king and Commons. Although the House of Commons contained many different strands of opinion, broadly speaking the majority were low church (against ritual), Calvinist, fiercely anti-Catholic and in favour of an actively interventionist Protestant foreign policy. In all except the last they were at odds with the Crown, and even the war against Spain was not carried out to their liking. There was, therefore, great scope for conflict (as the previous chapter demonstrated) but religious divisions gave the disputes between king and Commons a greater depth and a new bitterness.

The promotion of Arminians led to parliamentary attacks on those who were most outspoken in support of the royal prerogative. In 1627 Robert Sibthorpe declared that tribute was 'due to princes ... by the law of God as a sign of our subjection; by the law of nature, as the reward of their pains and protection' and 'by the law of nations as the sinews of the state's preservation'. This defence of the forced loan which many MPs regarded as illegal was not well received in the Commons, nor was the work of Roger Mainwaring who supported non-parliamentary taxation. Mainwaring was impeached, fined, imprisoned and barred from office, but after only a few weeks Charles pardoned him and gave him a new living. Such actions undermined parliament's trust in Charles as protector of their rights. John Selden neatly summed up the connection between religions and political beliefs:

> 1 The Puritans who will allow no freewill at all, but God does all, yet will allow the subject his liberty to do, or not to do, notwithstanding the king, the God upon earth. The Arminians, who hold we have freewill, yet say, when we come to the king there
> 5 must be all obedience, and no liberty to be stood for.

An attempt to heal religious divisions by holding a conference of Arminians and Puritans at York House in 1626 served merely to confirm that the Arminians had the backing of Buckingham and, by implication, of Charles. The Commons could protest at the direction of religious affairs but could do little to alter it. One MP expressed his frustration at seeing the Church altered around him. He accused Montagu of 'casting the odious and scandalous name of Puritans upon such His Majesty's loving subjects as conform themselves to the doctrine and ceremony of the Church of England'.

He objected so strongly to the label 'Puritan' because it implied being part of a sect. By the beginning of 1629 religion was taking precedence over all other business in the House of Commons. Charges of heterodoxy (holding opinions which were not orthodox) were made against Laud and a fellow Arminian, Bishop Neile. Francis Rous made a speech linking Arminianism with Catholicism and Spanish tyranny:

> I desire that we may look into the very belly and bowels of this Trojan horse to see if there not be men in it, ready to open the gates to Romish tyranny and Spanish monarchy; for an Arminian is the spawn of a papist.

More prosaically, Sir Robert Phelips suggested that 'Two sects are dangerously crept in to undermine king and kingdom; if not now prevented, the one ancient Popery, the other new Arminianism'. The Commons were in no doubt that true (Protestant) religion was under threat and that Arminianism was but the first step to undermine the ancient constitution, liberties and beliefs of Englishmen and to replace them with tyrannical Catholicism. They needed to look no further than the king's own court to see mass being openly celebrated for his wife surrounded by a cluster of foreign priests.

It was in this atmosphere of alarm that Eliot's three resolutions against Arminianism and tonnage and poundage were passed at the close of the 1629 parliament (see pages 78-9). The first resolution protested against 'innovation in religion'. Anyone who sought 'to extend or introduce Popery or Arminianism or other opinions disagreeing from the true and orthodox Church' would be regarded as a 'capital enemy to the king and Commonwealth'. Charles did not welcome such criticism of his handling of the Church where he was convinced that he knew best. He was determined to impose his own sense of order in religion.

7 The Religious Policy of the Personal Rule

It was in the 1630s, and especially after Laud became Archbishop of Canterbury in 1633, that the full impact of Arminianism was felt. In the 1620s, Arminian churchmen had been promoted and there had been suppression of Calvinist teaching but those who did not follow theological discussions or the affairs of parliament would have noticed little change. During the personal rule, however, alterations to the service were introduced which affected every parish in the kingdom. It became impossible to ignore the king's programme of reform and while some welcomed the new sense of reverence and structure that was imposed, others were deeply offended.

The changes were of two kinds: there was the suppression of preaching and there were changes to the conduct of services.

In many Puritan parishes the custom had grown up of having lectures on Sunday afternoons. These were little more than lengthy sermons, but if they were held after the regular morning service they did not need to conform to the established pattern of worship. Charles and Laud disliked preaching because it was difficult to control the content of sermons which might pose a threat to the authority of bishops. The Puritans sought to foster a more active spiritual life amongst their congregations and this could undermine the role of the church. Laud made his own views clear on the relative importance of the pulpit and the altar:

> The altar is the greatest place of God's residence upon earth. I say the greatest. Yea, greater than the pulpit, for there tis *Hoc est corpus meum* 'this is my body', but in the pulpit tis at most but *Hoc est verbum meum* 'this is my word'.

The attack upon preaching began immediately. In 1629 Charles ordered that catechizing (set question and answer sessions) replace sermons in parishes 'when and wheresoever there is no great cause apparent to break this ancient and profitable order'. Then it was ordered that each lecturer 'read divine service according to the liturgy printed by authority, in his surplice and hood before the congregation'. In the late 1620s a group of professional men in London had formed an association known as the 'feoffees for impropriations' with the aim of using charitable donations to buy up impropriations (the right to tithes) so that they could endow godly preaching. Land suppressed the feoffees which he feared might stir up unrest, although there is no evidence that the preachers were not solely concerned with the spiritual life of their congregations. One of the feoffees was so dispirited by this that he emigrated to the emerging Puritan colony in New England.

Services were made more uniform by insisting on a strict adherence to the prayer book, bowing by the congregation when the name of Jesus was spoken, and the wearing of a surplice by the minister. These had all been elements of the Elizabethan settlement, but had been ignored in many parishes. However, the most visible sign of the new beliefs was that the altar was to be railed in at the east end of the church. The Elizabethan prayer book stated that the altar table was to be kept at the east end and brought into the body of the church during services. In practice this was too inconvenient and each parish left the table in its preferred position. Laud not only wanted it permanently at the east end, but he also ordered it to be railed off, further creating the impression that the minister was a separate being cut off from his flock and able to mediate between them and God. It also implied that the eucharist was a sacrificial service, not merely a commemorative one, and was therefore like the Catholic mass. All of this was anathema to the Puritans as was the reissue of the Book of Sports with its implicit attack upon the sabbath. Stained glass, which smacked of the worship of images, was installed in some churches and organs and choir-stalls were established wherever possible.

Laud brought his motto of 'Thorough' (a determination to see that reforms were properly carried through and efficiently administered) to the enforcement of his ecclesiastical changes. All bishops were ordered to live in their diocese and to make regular visitations of the parishes. Clergy who were found to be infringing church laws were summoned before a church court or the Court of High Commission. High Commission was a prerogative court and therefore lay outside the jurisdiction of the ordinary common law courts. Laud used it to enforce obedience and it developed a fearsome reputation (demonstrated by its abolition in 1641 when parliament attacked what it saw as the abuses of the personal rule). This reputation was not diminished by the court's preference for forcing offenders into compliance rather than punishing them. Some clergy even fled rather than appear before the court.

8 Opposition to Arminianism

It is difficult to be certain how unpopular the religious changes were. In the absence of a parliament there was no forum for the public expression of widespread unrest. There was not universal dissatisfaction. Some liked the new ritual of their services and the Book of Sports was welcomed by many because it provided a chance to relax on the one non-working day of the week. But, undoubtedly, Laud's reforms offended and alienated large sections of the population who were profoundly uneasy at the direction religion was taking. In part this was a product of the feeling that the established Church they had grown up with was changing, and forcing those who had not altered their own beliefs into the position of non-conformists. It was now an offence to expound the 39 Articles in a predestination sense, although this was the orthodoxy of twenty years before. The Bishop of Salisbury voiced the bewilderment of many:

1 Why that should now be esteemed Puritan doctrine, which those
   held who have done our Church the greatest service in beating
   down Puritanism, or why men should be restrained from teaching
   that doctrine hereafter, which hitherto has been generally and
5 publicly maintained, (wiser men perhaps may) but I cannot
   understand.

Emigration to New England increased markedly in the 1630s and was seriously considered by John Pym amongst others. For some it seemed the only answer in an England which was moving in a popish direction without anyone being able to resist. There were Puritan pamphlets in which bishops were described as 'tigers', 'vipers', 'bloodsuckers', and 'cruel stepfathers of the church', but detection of the author could result in severe punishment. The most notorious case was that of William Prynne, a lawyer, Henry Burton, a clergyman, and John Bastwick, a doctor. They had all published attacks on the Church and in 1637 were tried in Star Chamber, found guilty and condemned to a gruesome punishment. Their ears were cut off in the pillory, they had to pay a heavy fine and were sentenced to life imprisonment.

Much of the outrage at Prynne, Burton and Bastwick's punishment was caused not because they were Puritan pamphleteers but because they were gentlemen who ought not to have been subjected to such a degrading punishment. This was another feature of the opposition to Laud. He was seen to be attacking the position and property rights of the gentry, an attack which was felt all the more keenly because Laud himself was not a member of the gentry - his father was a cloth merchant. Prynne called him 'a little, low, red-faced man'. Laud was anxious to restore the wealth of the Church in order to improve the status of the clergy. Restrictions were put on the terms which ecclesiastical landlords could offer to their tenants. This was designed to stop the practice where bishops would offer a long lease on a low rent in return for a high entry fine, thus impoverishing future clergy for their own gain. The tenants who lost out were usually from the gentry. Laud also made unsuccessful attempts to recover impropriations (the right to collect tithes) to provide more money for clergy stipends. This could only be done at the expense of the gentry because they were the ones who had bought up the impropriations.

Another, perhaps more surprising, reason for the gentry to dislike Arminianism was that it blurred social distinctions which Puritanism tended to highlight. For example, in Norwich diocese pews were ordered to be of uniform size so as not to block the view of the altar. This offended the leaders of local communities who sought to underline their importance by having elaborate pews. It was the gentry who were so opposed to the reissue of the Book of Sports because it threatened their law enforcement role by potentially encouraging disorder through the sanction it gave to such supposedly immoral pursuits as dancing. However, Arminianism provoked the greatest opposition, not because of what it did but because of what it appeared to lead to. The fear of popery was greatly increased by the new ceremonial of Arminianism and the open acceptance of Catholics at court gave rise to rumours of a popish plot to take over the country.

9 Charles I and the Catholics

Charles was not a religious fanatic and he was prepared to tolerate different theological views from his own, provided that those who held them maintained outward conformity and submission. He was reported to believe that 'so long as a man believed in Christ he could save his soul whatever religion he was born baptized and bred'. Not everyone felt able to compromise their beliefs by outward conformity and the largest group so affected were the Catholics. A dual standard was practised throughout Charles's reign. On the one hand, Catholics in the country were subjected to ever-greater financial burdens as recusancy fines were rigorously enforced. On the other hand, Catholic worship was openly allowed at court and English people were permitted to attend mass in Henrietta Maria's or one of the foreign ambassador's chapels. There were a number of highly visible conversions among the aristocracy and it seemed as if Catholicism was developing its hold at the very heart of English society.

The question of perception was very important. However much Charles ordered recusancy fines to be enforced, Jesuits to be detained, and those who protected them to be punished, the impression remained in the country that the government inclined to popery. Laud's habit of calling the clergy 'priests' summed up the religious divide. If the government favoured Catholics it could not protect the country against a popish plot. This was a fear which seemed all too plausible given Catholic success in the Thirty Years War up to 1630 and the influence of the queen. Ironically, Laud was one of the fiercest opponents of Court Catholicism but it was not only the Protestants who failed to understand his position. The Pope even offered him a cardinal's hat, which he indignantly turned down.

The permissive attitude towards Catholicism at court was shown in a number of ways. A series of papal envoys from 1634 onwards drew attention to the presence of Catholics around the king. Many of Charles's ministers, for example Lord Treasurer Weston and Sir Francis Cottington, were open or secret Catholics. Henrietta Maria came to exercise increasing influence as the 1630s progressed. Charles's foreign policy of aligning himself with Catholic powers, first France and then Spain, created more worries about the government's intentions. In no area did the king appear to be supporting the Protestant religion. In these circumstances perhaps it is not surprising that rumours spread of a popish plot to undermine true religion and liberty.

a) Anti-Popery and the Popish Plot

An irrational fear of Catholicism lay just below the surface of English society in the seventeenth century. This had little to do with the actual numbers of Catholics in the country, who numbered perhaps 60,000 in 1640 out of population of over three million. It had more to do with the feeling that Protestants were under threat. The most popular book at this time, apart from the Bible, was Foxe's *Book of Martyrs* which dwelt in grisly detail on the torments of Protestants in the sixteenth century. The dread that Catholics might once again seize control of England was increased by a series of alarms from the 1580s onwards - the Armada, the Gunpowder Plot, and invasion scares in the 1620s when England was at war with France and Spain. Before 1625 these threats were all external, either from abroad or from those who felt excluded from the political process. In Charles I's reign there was a new fear that Catholicism had infected the very heart of government and the idea of a conspiracy to destroy the liberties and religion of the country gained widespread currency.

Apprehension increased from 1637 as Catholic influence on policy seemed undeniable. Charles had embarked on a misguided attempt to force the Scots to accept a prayer book which they regarded as popish. At the same time he was negotiating with Catholic Spain for money to suppress his Protestant Scottish subjects. These negotiations came to nothing but they were widely known about. Once war against the Scots was underway, Charles seemed more interested in getting military support from Catholics in Ireland and Scotland and allowing Henrietta Maria to ask for donations from the English Catholic community than in seeking the support of his Protestant English parliament. It seemed as if the traditional alliance of king and parliament at times of crisis was under threat and with it the entire English constitution. The arrival of the Catholic Queen Mother, Marie de Medici, at the height of the Scottish crisis could not have been worse timed, especially as Charles was away in the north. Even his return did little to calm nerves because it coincided with the arrival of a large Spanish fleet sailing towards

Dunkirk which led to fears of invasion.

It was in this mood of heightened religious tension that the Short Parliament met in April 1640. Its abrupt dissolution and the presence of three Spanish envoys at court led to rumours that the parliament had fallen because of a popish plot and speculations ran riot: some claimed that Charles had converted, the mayor of Norwich reported a tip-off that the city was to be attacked by 12,000 papists, and Londoners petitioned that Catholics should be forced to wear 'distinguishing clothes'.

The atmosphere of hysteria in the summer of 1640, generated by fears of a popish plot, destroyed the chance of a moderate and accommodating parliament. John Pym, in the first speech in the Commons in November, set the tone of the debates. There is 'a design to alter the kingdom both in religion, and government. This is the highest of treason'. Unstated but implicit in what he said was that if the policies were the king's then he was guilty of treason. The tragedy for Charles was that there was no popish plot. His commitment to the Protestant religion was as strong as most of his subjects although he interpreted that religion in a manner that many of them found incomprehensible. However, Charles lacked the common touch and could not explain his policies or beliefs in a way that would allay fears about the intentions or direction of the government.

10 The Drive for Uniformity: Ireland and Scotland, 1625-40

Charles was determined to achieve religious uniformity in his three kingdoms. This required a tactful and cautious approach but such methods were alien to Charles. As James had already discovered, religion aroused strong passions, and uniformity should have been seen as a long-term aspiration rather than an immediate goal. The task in Charles's reign was made more difficult because he was attempting to make significant changes to the religion of each of his three kingdoms. His anti-Calvinist interpretation of the 39 Articles created opposition even in England, and the Scottish and Irish Churches were more firmly Calvinist than their English counterpart. In these circumstances, any attempt to introduce major religious changes would be full of difficulty.

a) Ireland

In Ireland, Charles concentrated his reforms on the established church, which was modelled on the Church of England. The Catholics were allowed to practise their religion unmolested because the new Lord Deputy Wentworth saw the Presbyterian settlers in Ulster as more of a threat. Therefore, he directed his reforms at the Church of Ireland to bring it closer to the practices prevailing in England. In this way he hoped to limit the influence of the Presbyterians. The Irish Church had strongly Calvinist beliefs, no doubt because of the need to assert itself against the Catholic majority. Arminians were appointed to vacant bishoprics often in opposition to the wishes of the Calvinist Archbishop Ussher of Armagh. The imposition of Arminian ceremonialism was deeply unpopular with the Irish Church but it had no means of making an effective protest. Puritan opposition was crushed by the Court of High Commission which was set up in 1634. Those who refused to conform lost their livings.

Others who might have supported the reforms were alienated by Wentworth's campaign to win back church lands which was intended to alleviate the poverty of the clergy. Since the Reformation most of the Church's wealth had fallen into the hands of laymen. The attack on their property rights made Wentworth influential enemies such as the Earl of Cork. Church reform united many different groups against the government and it was suggested that Wentworth would be the man most likely to overturn the Protestant cause.

b) Scotland

In Scotland, Presbyterianism was supported by the vast majority of the population. The Scottish Church was organised in a different way from the Church of England. Although James had imposed bishops onto the already existing system of assemblies, the latter remained an important part of Church government. Successful reform in Scotland would require close consultation, especially with the highly important general assembly. This was not Charles's style and he displayed insensitivity almost immediately. In 1626, he issued a proclamation commanding observation of the Articles of Perth and he sent personal instructions for kneeling at communion. This clearly demonstrated what little understanding he had of how repugnant such an order was to the Scots.

In 1633, on his first visit to Scotland since becoming king, Charles and Laud were shocked at how plain the churches were. They were completely devoid of ornament. The two men returned to England determined to make Scottish worship conform more closely to their ideas of decency and reverence. On instructions from the king, the Scottish bishops drew up a Book of Common Prayer and canons 'for the uniformity of ... discipline'. The canons laid down east-end tables, kneeling, and confession, which caused much offence. But even worse was the lack of consultation with the clergy and the imposition of the canons by royal decree. Ominously, the canons required obedience on pain of excommunication to a prayer book that no one had seen because it was not yet completed. Understandably, there were grave fears about what the book would contain and rumours were widespread that it was full of 'popish rites'. This was not true and the bishops had gone to some trouble to remove potentially offensive words, such as 'priest' which appeared in the English prayerbook, from the version prepared for use in Scotland. Laud believed there was 'no one thing in that Book which may not stand with the conscience of a right good Protestant' but the Scots were not prepared to give it a fair trial. It was seen as an alien English imposition which would lead the Scots into error. A petition of 1637 condemned it for sowing 'the seeds of divers superstitions, idolatry and false doctrine, contrary to the true religion established within this realm'. The involvement of the bishops in the prayerbook's preparation damaged their already weak position. Unwittingly, at a stroke, Charles had undone James's reforms and his subsequent handling of the affair was to drive a wedge between the Scottish and English Churches. The National Covenant which was drawn up to oppose the prayerbook bound its subscribers to maintain the true faith of the Kirk of Scotland against the 'innovations and evils which have no warrant of the word of God: and do sensibly tend to the re-establishing of the popish religion and tyranny, and to the subversion and ruin of our liberties, laws and estates'.

The full story of the Covenant and the subsequent Bishops' Wars will be told in the next chapter. Here it will suffice to point out that it was Charles's ill-judged religious policy in Scotland which brought an end to the personal rule, and that it was fears about religion in England which poisoned the atmosphere of the Long Parliament, making an accommodation between king and Commons almost impossible to achieve. The Convocation of 1640 only added to the fears for the future.

11 Convocation and the Canons of 1640

It was customary for a convocation of clergy in England to be summoned at the same time as a parliament and one had duly met while the Short Parliament was in session. Charles gave it a licence to draw up canons for the direction and government of the Church for the first time since 1606. Thus far was uncontroversial, but there were aspects of this convocation which made people uneasy. First, the clergy immediately granted six subsidies to the king while their secular counterparts were discussing grievances. Secondly, the changes in the Church since 1606 meant that parliament wished to assert its authority in religious matters and was unwilling to leave the direction of the Church entirely to convocation. Thirdly, convocation continued to sit after the dissolution of parliament in defiance of precedence which meant that their actions had a dubious legality. Finally, the canons which convocation drew up caused further problems.

Laud hoped the canons would promote peace in the Church. They resolutely condemned popery and were deliberately moderate: the position of the table under the east window was declared to be 'in its own nature indifferent'. Probably intended in the same moderate spirit was an oath for the preventing of all innovations in the doctrine and

This Canons feal'd, well forg'd, not made of lead,
Give fire, O noe I will breake and strike vs dead,

That I A.B. doe fweare that I doe approve the Doctrine and Difcipline or Government eſtabliſhed in the Church of England, as containing all things neceſſary to Salvation, And that I will not endeavour by my ſelfe or any other, directly or indirectly to bring in any Popiſh Doctrine, contrary to that which is ſo eſtabliſhed: Nor will I ever give my conſent to alter the Government of this Church, by Archbiſhops, Biſhops, Deanes, and Arch Deacons &c as it ſtands now eſtabliſhed, and as by right it ought to ſtand: Nor yet ever to ſubject it to the uſurpations and ſuperſtitions of the Sea of Rome, And all theſe things I doe plainly and ſincerely acknowledge and ſweare, according to the plain and common ſence, and underſtanding of the ſame words, without any equivocation or mentall evaſion, or ſecret reſervation whatſoever. And this I doe heartily, willingly and truly, upon the faith of a Chriſtian: So help me God in Ieſus Chriſt,

Prime, lay the Trayne, thus you must mount, and levell,
    then ſhall we gett the day, *but freind the Devill,*
Turne, wheele about, take tyme, and stand your ground,
    this Canon cannot faile, *but tis not sound,*
Feare not, weel cast it, tis a desperate case,
    weel sweare it, and enjoyne it, *but tis base,*
The Mettalls brittle, and tis ram'd so hard,
    with an *Oath* &c: that hath fowly marr'd
All our designes, that now we have no hope
    but in the service of *our Lord the Pope,*
Dissolve the Rout, each man vnto his calling
    which had we kept, we had not now beene falling

A satire against Archbishop Laud by Wenceslaus Hollar, 1640

government of the Church. It was supposed to 'secure all men against any suspicion of revolt to Popery' and required all clergy to swear that they approved 'the doctrine and discipline, or government established in the Church of England, as containing all things necessary for salvation' and that they would not consent to alter 'the government of this church by archbishops, bishops, deans and archdeacons etc'.

This oath misfired disastrously. Instead of reassuring people that the church was safe in the king's hands, the 'etc' was interpreted to mean the Pope and the 'etcetera oath', as it became known, was seen as part of a plot to destroy the Protestant Church and convert it to Rome. Puritan pamphlets were produced showing Laud setting fire to a cannon which then exploded in his face. The level of outrage was such that the oath had to be abandoned. Far from bringing peace to the Church, convocation and its aftermath merely inflamed already heated passions and drove the two sides further apart into mutual incomprehension.

12 Conclusion

Religious passions which had been kept in check for over half a century, flared up in the 1630s and were a major contributor in the bitterness which led to civil war. Could religious strife have been avoided in England at a time when the continent was engaged in a fierce struggle between Catholic and Protestant? Were Charles I and Laud entirely responsible for the re-appearance of religion as a key point of conflict by their apparent inability to see how their actions would be interpreted?

Religious differences under James I had been successfully contained. Was this because much of his reign coincided with a period of relative calm in Europe? Or was it because James's policy towards the Church was designed to avoid conflict and not to promote it? James did not give much away to the Puritans but he was prepared to listen to their concerns. His appointments to the bench of bishops reflected the prevailing orthodoxy in the Church. In Scotland, he proceeded with tact and caution and he understood the theological differences between different strands of opinion.

Charles I was convinced that he was right and that opposition to him was misguided or sinful. Religion which deals with ultimate questions does not lend itself to compromise. The absolute claims made by religious groups that they had a monopoly of the truth created a climate of intolerance. Charles might have been able to defuse this situation if he had not been determined to pursue a form of Anglicanism that had many of the trappings of Catholicism. For a sizeable minority of his subjects, attendance at Arminian services threatened their immortal souls. Contrast the ways in which James I and Charles I handled the Church. How different would the outcome have been if James had remained king for another fifteen years?

Making notes on 'Religion, 1603-40'

This chapter is concerned with ideas as much as with events. Your notes should aim to give you a clear understanding of the points at issue. Try to imagine yourself back in the seventeenth century with its very limited conception of science when religious questions were a matter of life and death. What place did religion have in most people's lives? Make sure you can explain the difference between an Arminian, a Puritan and a member of the mainstream of the Church of England. What lay behind the fear of the Catholics? Do you see why the Scots were so determined to preserve their religious settlement? Once you have a real understanding of the answers to these questions, it will be much easier to appreciate why people acted as they did.

Use the following headings and questions as a framework for your notes.

1   The Position in 1603
2   James I and the Catholics
2.1 The Gunpowder Plot
3   James I and the Puritans
    What did the Puritans want?
3.1 The Hampton Court Conference
    Explain its failure
3.2 The Enforcement of Conformity
4   Religious Divisions Reappear
    What was Arminianism?

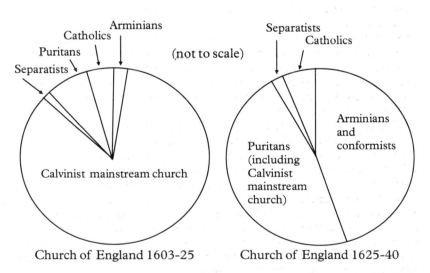

Church of England 1603-25   Church of England 1625-40

Summary - Religion, 1603-40

Answering essay questions on 'Religion, 1603-40'

1   'James I's main success was the way he handled religious non-conformity.' Do you agree?
2   How far were the religious problems of James I's reign the result of the Hampton Court Conference?
3   In what ways did the religious policies of Charles I differ from those of James I?
4   Discuss the effect of the increasing influence of Arminians in the church and at court between 1625 and 1640.
5   To what extent was the unpopularity of Charles I's personal rule the result of the actions and policies of William Laud?

You will see that the first two questions make opposite assumptions about the success of James I's religious policy. This should make it obvious that the examiners do not expect you to agree with the wording of a question. Sometimes a question will be set with the deliberate intention of being provocative. Your task is to show the ways in which the assertion in the question is wrong and to back up your points with evidence. It can often be helpful to undertake an essay title whose assumptions you disagree with because it encourages you to think out a clear line of argument to refute the preconceptions of the question.

Questions 1 and 5 require you to think not just about religion but also about the other issues involved in James and Charles's success or failure. However the main focus of the essay should continue to be religion. Question 5 has been included here for ease of reference but you will need to study chapter 7 before you can answer it fully.

Source-based questions on 'Religion, 1603-40'

1 Puritans and Arminians
Carefully read the extracts from John Selden, given on page 96 and from Francis Rous, given on page 96. Answer the following questions.
a)   What is the 'freewill' to which Selden refers? (2 marks)
b)   Do you think Selden preferred the Puritans or the Arminians? Give reasons for your answer. (3 marks)
c)   By using the term 'Trojan horse', what is Rous implying about Arminianism? (2 marks)
d)   Show how Rous's use of language might turn people against Arminianism. (3 marks)

2 William Laud and the Altar
Study Laud's views on the altar and the pulpit, given on page 97. Answer the following questions.
a)   What reasons does Laud give for attaching such importance to the altar? (2 marks)
b)   In what ways do Laud's views on the altar and the pulpit illustrate Arminian policy in the 1630s? (5 marks)
c)   In what ways would a Puritan have disagreed with Laud's views? (3 marks)

3 Opposition to Arminianism
Carefully read the Bishop of Salisbury's complaint (page 99) about the changing definition of a Puritan. Answer the following questions.
a)   Explain the confusion of the Bishop of Salisbury. (3 marks)
b)   What does this extract reveal about mainstream church attitudes to Charles's religious policies? (2 marks)
c)   In what ways does the extract indicate that the meaning of the word 'Puritan' has changed since James's reign? (3 marks)
Study the cartoon on Archbishop Laud and the Canons of 1640. Answer the following questions.
d)   What does the rhyme under the picture fear the oath was trying to promote? (2 marks)
e)   How does the wording of the oath (given above the picture) reveal that the fears of the cartoon and rhyme were misplaced? (2 marks)
f)   In what ways would the message of the cartoon be different for a literate and illiterate reader? (3 marks)

CHAPTER 7

The Personal Rule of Charles I, 1629–40

The personal rule was the period of eleven years when Charles I governed the country without recourse to parliament. It was not uncommon to have long intervals between parliaments. James I had managed from 1610 to 1621 with only the abortive Addled Parliament of 1614. However, historians have seen the 1630s as a distinct period because, as the decade progressed, Charles became resolved to do without parliament altogether. This resolve was not apparent in March 1629 when his third parliament was dissolved because Charles announced that he would call another one

> 1 when our people shall see more clearly into our intentions and actions, when such as have bred this interruption shall have received their condign [deserved] punishment, and those who are misled by them and by such ill reports as are raised upon this
> 5 occasion shall come to a better understanding of us and themselves.

It was obvious that Charles was angry at the failure of the third parliament and especially at the scenes which preceded its dissolution, but he clearly anticipated calling another one. There was widespread apprehension about the bad feeling between king and Commons. One observer wrote that 'not only all mouths are stopped, but the parliament doors sealed for many years', but this was not a universal view and it was expected that there would be another parliament when tempers had cooled. In fact, the king's attitude hardened over the next decade and it was only a grave national emergency caused by the folly of Charles's policy in Scotland which prompted the recall of parliament in 1640. What caused a prince, whom one contemporary described as 'bred in parliaments', to turn his back on them and what was the role of parliament in the governing of the country that the king could afford to dispense with it for eleven years?

1 Charles and Parliament

Charles and parliament, especially the House of Commons, began the reign with mutual high hopes. Yet in March 1629 Contarini, the Venetian ambassador, wrote

> 1 Parliament is dissolved in anger, and without deciding anything ...
> The courtiers are very disconsolate, foreseeing that they will remain a long time in need, without money, as they have been for

many months. The kingdom is furious against the Treasurer, and
5 bears the king very little love … What matters is that parliament has
retained the full possession of its privileges without yielding a jot,
for on the last two occasions the king has always yielded
something. If he returns again he will have to do the same, and if he
does not, which many believe to be his determination in order not
10 to lose his crown, it will be a difficult matter to find money.

In four short years the trust between the Commons and their sovereign
had been dissipated never to return. Contarini identified the two main
points of dispute, money and parliamentary privilege, but these issues in
themselves were symptoms and not the cause of the breakdown between
king and parliament. The underlying causes went deeper and there were
shortcomings on both sides.

The House of Commons saw the king pursuing policies in religion,
foreign affairs and finance which required explanation if they were ever
to command widespread support. Many of the policies favoured by
Charles reversed the practice of several decades, especially friendship
with Spain and Arminianism. Great tact was needed in the presentation
of these policies, but there was no effective management of
parliamentary debates provided by the court. Money was requested, but
the reasons for the crown's pressing financial requirements were not
spelt out. The absence of leadership from the crown prompted others
who opposed the direction of royal policy to take the lead. Parliament
became a means of applying pressure to the king by men such as the
Earls of Warwick and Pembroke who were excluded from influence at
court by the all-powerful position of the Duke of Buckingham.

Lesser men also found their route to advancement blocked by
Buckingham's control of patronage and were driven into opposition.
MPs, including Sir Thomas Wentworth and Sir Edward Coke, who
wished to enter royal service vented their frustration and bitterness in
the Commons and directed debates in the House in a manner that was
often hostile to the crown. That this hostility could be a product of
frustration at exclusion from power seems to be borne out by the
example of Wentworth. He led the debates over the Petition of Right but
then became one of Charles's most loyal servants when he was taken
into the Privy Council and given the presidency of the Council of the
North in 1628.

Lack of royal leadership coupled with innovatory policies and a
desperate financial crisis strained relations between king and Commons
and led the latter to adopt procedures which Charles could justifiably
regard as going beyond the bounds of tradition. Parliament had given its
sanction for the war against Spain and could therefore have been
expected to provide sufficient finance to wage it successfully. However,
the Commons refused to do this because of their uncertainty about what
the money would be used for and because the need for the huge sums

requested was not adequately explained. Charles responded by raising money in whatever way he could - by the forced loan and by continuing to collect tonnage and poundage after the period agreed by parliament.

The Petition of Right and the assassination of Buckingham increased the suspicions of both king and Commons. Charles would never forgive or forget that the murderer claimed to have been inspired by the Petition of Right, even though he had acknowledged that the duke was 'the only wall of separation between us and our people'. When the Commons again refused, in 1629, to grant him tonnage and poundage for life, Charles was persuaded that he could dispense with parliament. Eliot's outburst provided the perfect justification and enabled Charles to put the blame for the breakdown in relations between himself and the Commons firmly on the shoulders of a few ill-disposed malcontents. Eliot himself was to die, unrepentant, in the Tower in 1632. The other eight members who had taken part in the demonstration gradually submitted to the king, although two were not released until the eve of the Short Parliament in 1640. Both king and Commons could claim with some justification that their behaviour was in accordance with tradition and that it was the other who was responsible for the breakdown in relations. What difference would the absence of parliament make to the functioning of government?

In the short term the answer was 'very little'. James I had ruled successfully from 1610 to 1621 with only the abortive Addled Parliament in 1614. Statute laws were comparatively rare and parliament did not formulate policy. The real importance of regular sessions was more symbolic. In a society with relatively primitive means of communication, an institution which brought the monarch into contact with representatives of his people so that he could hear their requests and fears had enormous value. Parliament acted as a safety valve. Serious unease could be expressed about the direction of royal policy without undue danger of reprisals by the sovereign, because a tradition of free speech in parliament had gradually been established. The king would then know that he must either modify his policies or explain them so that they became more acceptable if he did not wish to face further unrest. This was crucial in the 1630s because Charles was pursuing a whole range of policies which were deeply unpopular.

Debates about the direction of affairs were held in the Privy Council and factions would develop supporting different policies, such as the pro-Spanish Howard faction under James I. The suppression of effective discussion in the Privy Council during the years of Buckingham's ascendency distorted the traditional system and meant parliament became the only arena for expressing dissent. This new opposition role came at a time when the crown was introducing innovatory and unpopular changes in religion and foreign policy. When this was combined with a long-term financial crisis the results were explosive. No longer did Charles feel at his most powerful in parliament. The House of

Commons had become a severe critic of the government and the king no longer considered it worth the struggle to win its approval.

2 Charles's Government

a) Character

Earlier this century it was fashionable to see the Personal Rule as 'the Eleven Years Tyranny.' Charles was suspected of trying to establish absolutist government on the continental model. There are several reasons why this interpretation can no longer be supported. It is clear that Charles had little interest in politics. A frequent comment on papers sent to him for a decision was 'Do it if you find it suit my service'. It is therefore very unlikely that the decision to rule without parliament had been part of a grand strategy. It is much more probable that it was the product of extreme frustration caused by the fact that parliament would not give him what he wanted. Charles was careful to remain within the law even if sometimes he strained its interpretation. His actions had to be seen to be legal because without the co-operation of the county elites royal authority could not be sustained.

b) The Privy Council

The main organ of government was the Privy Council, which met twice weekly. The Privy Council handled the routine business of government and much of what it dealt with was mundane. In the 1630s the administration of business was improved by the creation of committees to deal with different aspects of the Council's work such as Scotland, Ireland and trade. When faced by a crisis the Privy Council could respond well, as the efficient supervision of ship money demonstrates. However, more routine affairs were liable to suffer from the under-staffing of the clerks. There was always too much work to be done and this left little opportunity for the initiation of policy or of long-term strategies. The Book of Orders (see page 114) is a good example of a worthy attempt by the government to tackle a social problem which foundered for want of adequate direction.

Although the Privy Council was essential for the smooth running of the country, its other function - of advising the monarch - was much less important in the 1630s. Charles rarely attended its meetings, he was present on average once a month, and major policy decisions were usually made by the king after consultation with a group of close associates who shared his religious and political beliefs.

c) Local Government

At the other end of the chain of command from the Privy Council were the Justices of the Peace (JPs) of whom there were approximately 50 in each county. There were no paid permanent royal agents in the counties. Everything rested on the co-operation of the Justices who were chosen by the king from among the leading gentry. It was considered a real honour to be given a commission of the peace and it was a mark of status in the county community. Justices of the Peace had a wide-ranging brief. They met four times a year in the principal town of each county at the Quarter Sessions. These Sessions provided both a court of law and an administrative forum, which could ensure that the localities were being well run. It was also an occasion to pass on directives from the Privy Council. The communication between central and local government was erratic. It was difficult to maintain sustained control for long periods. Once the immediate point of concern had been dealt with, the Justices were free to continue to run their localities much as they chose.

Some historians have argued that the relationship between central and local government was typically illustrated by the administration of poor relief through the Book of Orders of January 1631. The harvest of 1630 was the worst of the early Stuart period and with food riots in the worst affected parts of the West Country, there were fears of more unrest unless effective poor relief could be organised. The Privy Council, therefore, revived a scheme of the Earl of Manchester from 1620. The Book of Orders it published consisted of eight orders and twelve directions. The orders instructed justices to supervise local officers such as constables every month and to make quarterly reports to the sheriff who would pass them via the assize judges to the Privy Council. The directions were to see that justices prevented vagrancy, placed poor children in apprenticeships, punished delinquents, put the idle to work and kept the roads repaired. Initially, the Book was successful in solving the immediate crisis. Thereafter, the reports sent in by Justices became so vague as to be effectively useless in assessing the true state of their localities.

For a long time historians thought of the Book of Orders as indicating an innovatory approach to local government which sought to alter its relationship with the centre and apply more effective control. However, it is now judged that it was in a long tradition of concern for the poor whom, it was feared, would become a social menace without proper relief. The only unusual feature of the Book was in its requirement for regular reports which Justices often ignored. In other respects the Orders demonstrated the short-term strategy of early Stuart economic policy - alleviating the effects of a crisis without attempting to tackle its causes. As with finance, it was easier to keep to the system that already existed.

3 The Court

The court of Charles I mirrored the king's personality. It was formal, dignified and elegant. It was also remote, inward-looking and rigid. Charles was not an intellectual and did not enjoy vigorous debate, so he surrounded himself with men who shared his interests and beliefs. He was also very high-minded. The contrast with the court of James I could not have been more extreme. A contemporary courtier, Lucy Hutchinson, put it thus:

> The face of the court was much changed in the king, for King Charles was temperate, chaste and serious, so that the fools and bawds, mimics and catamites of the former court, grew out of fashion.

Charles I with Henrietta Maria and Prince Charles and Princess Mary by Van Dyck, 1632

The familiarity of James's court which had repelled many, was replaced by strict directives about who was allowed access to the Privy Chamber, Presence Chamber and Bed Chamber, and the royal family's public acts, such as eating, were governed by rigid rules of etiquette, laying down, for example, the distance to be kept from the royal family and the necessity of serving the king on bended knee. Charles was condemned to eating lukewarm food as a result. To escape from the stifling formality of court ritual, Charles indulged his great passion of hunting whenever he had the opportunity. The royal household was in constant motion between the various royal palaces, but unlike Elizabeth, Charles did not seek to win his people's love by showing himself to them. Instead, he tried to keep himself as private as possible.

At the heart of the court was the royal family and this absorbed much of Charles's emotional energy. After its unfortunate beginning, his marriage to Henrietta Maria had turned into a warm and loving relationship and the birth of his children undoubtedly gave Charles deep satisfaction. His eldest son, Charles, was born in 1630 and seven other children followed in the years to 1644. The other consuming interest of Charles's life was patronage of the visual arts. He devoted more of his time and energy in the 1630s to developing his art collection than to any other activity. Once, when engaged in critical and delicate negotiations over support for the Palatine, Viscount Dorchester found him rearranging his busts of Roman emperors. Charles undoubtedly created one of the finest collections of Renaissance art ever made. At his death, according to one estimate, there were 1,760 paintings and many sculptures in the royal collection. He had excellent taste and could distinguish the hand of a master from that of his assistants. He bought with discretion and loved to discuss art. It is no coincidence that in 1629 the Spanish chose the painter Rubens to open negotiations for peace.

Unfortunately, this apparently harmless, if expensive, activity was seen by many in a more sinister light. Charles's patronage of Catholics such as Rubens, who painted the ceilings of the Banqueting House in Whitehall, and Bernini, who made a bust of the king, aroused deep suspicion. William Prynne saw the negotiations with Bernini which were assisted by the Pope's nephew, Cardinal Barberini, as part of a plot 'to seduce the king with pictures, antiquities, images and other vanities bought from Rome'. Even the patronage of the architect Inigo Jones could be regarded with distrust because his Palladian style was regarded as profoundly un-English and the purposes to which his buildings were put was also a cause for disapproval. For example, he built chapels at Somerset House and in St James' Palace where the queen and many courtiers heard mass. The Banqueting House was used for masques which were seen as expensive and immoral imports from France and Italy. Both of the early Stuarts took great delight in masques - elaborate plays full of symbolism which were performed only once at enormous cost. Charles and Henrietta Maria liked to take part in the masques,

Palatium Regis prope Londinum, *vulgo* White-hall.

Whitehall Palace from the river, etching by Wenceslaus Hollar, 1647, showing the Banqueting Hall by Inigo Jones

their appearance usually heralding order brought out of chaos - a role the king believed he performed in real life. Royal participation in such frivolous activities was regarded with deep suspicion, especially by those such as Prynne who were of a Puritan persuasion. It seemed to indicate a leaning towards the supposed immorality of Catholicism and contributed to the sense of unease about the court. This identification of Charles's artistic tastes with the world of the Counter-Reformation would not have been so serious if it had not been linked to innovatory policies in religion and foreign policy. Fears grew that the court was seeking to introduce Catholicism by means of Arminianism, and to forge an alliance with Spain, thus abandoning the Protestant cause and with it the Palatinate. Such fears were increased because of the existence of the 'political court', Charles's inner ring of advisers who shared his artistic, political and cultural outlooks. Those who believed in the political orthodoxy of the previous half century - the alliance with the Dutch against Spain, the participation of parliament, and the established Calvinism of the English Church - found themselves increasingly cut off from influence. Sir Thomas Roe, a fervent supporter of the Protestant cause who was therefore excluded from government service, wrote ironically 'We cannot say there is any faction in England. All goes one way and I know not the wit of it'.

The political court was labelled by contemporaries as the 'Spanish faction'. All favoured alliance with Spain and with the exception of the king, Laud and Wentworth, the members of the political court preferred the Roman Catholic Church although they mostly preserved outward conformity to the Church of England - Weston converted on his death bed in 1635. These attitudes could only hope to flourish in the absence of parliament and so the king was confirmed in his decision to rule alone.

4 Rule without Parliament

The precipitate dissolution of the third parliament left Charles in a dire financial predicament. He did not have a parliamentary grant, and customs revenue was reduced both by the war and by many merchants' refusal to pay tonnage and poundage. Most seriously of all, the country was still at war with the two major powers of Europe. All of these required some action. Peace negotiations were speedily concluded with France in 1629 and with Spain in 1630. The boycott of trade by merchants gradually collapsed as it became apparent that there would not be another parliament for some time and that their livelihood would suffer unless they resumed normal trading.

Charles had abandoned the idea of a parliamentary subsidy so he had to find alternative means of raising revenue. It was important to avoid policies which could be seen as illegal or contrary to custom because the king could not afford to jeopardize the support of the justices of the peace and other local officials on whom his government depended. This left few options for Lord Treasurer Weston who was driven to exploit obscure prerogative rights and to trying to curb royal expenditure. He was assisted in his task of restoring royal finances by the recovery of customs revenue.

5 Finance

a) Customs Revenue

The advent of peace brought great commercial opportunities in a Europe which was still torn apart by war and English merchants lost no time in seizing them. They traded, among other things, in arms, foodstuffs, and military and naval supplies. These were particularly important for the Spanish war effort because their land routes to northern Europe had been blocked by the war and the sea-route or 'English road' became vital. With the Dutch excluded, England obtained a near monopoly of the Iberian trade as well as continuing to trade with the North. English overseas trade reached unprecedented heights of prosperity in the 1630s and there was a corresponding increase in crown revenue, two-thirds of which was accounted for by customs. This increase meant that by the end of 1630s Charles was effectively solvent, but in 1629, faced with a debt of one million pounds, with no money for day-to-day expenditure, more urgent solutions were required.

b) Economies

Weston's main aim was to try to curb royal expenditure. The royal household accounted for £260,000 a year, which was about 40 per cent of the king's income. This was partly because of its sheer size. It employed between 1,800 and 2,600 people (with their dependents they would have amounted to the population of a town almost the size of Exeter or Norwich). But it was not only the numbers involved, there was also appalling waste. The king had 24 meat dishes twice daily. Each day's ration allowance of £25 5s 4d would have kept 1,962 people for a whole year! Clearly there was considerable scope for cost cutting: restricting the diet for the household to what the royal family and their immediate attendants could actually eat would have released £80-90,000 a year for other purposes. But reform was too expensive politically. Too many of the king's servants considered it their right to supplement their income from the household accounts either through an excessive ration allowance or through selling the waste. They had a vested interest in the system continuing unchanged. Weston managed to halt the upward curve of expenditure but there were few significant economies and no structural reform of the king's finances was undertaken. That the crown was nearly solvent at his death in 1635 owes more to increasing customs revenue and to money from prerogative rights than it does to any success in tackling waste.

c) Prerogative Rights

To be able to dispense with parliament permanently would have required a radical overhaul of royal finance. This might have had serious political repercussions. Official salaries were so low that office-holders relied on the perks which went with their jobs, such as holding the freehold of an office which gave them an income for life, or charging fees to would-be clients. Any attempt to attack these privileges would have involved a dangerous erosion of support amongst the very people upon whom the king depended to carry out his instructions. Instead, Weston adopted a series of fund-raising measures using prerogative rights which had fallen into disuse. These are collectively known as 'fiscal feudalism'. There was a whole series of different ways of raising money, one of the most successful of which was distraint of knighthood. In theory, every man with an income of more than £40 per annum was supposed to present himself at the coronation to be knighted. Inflation had eroded the value of £40 and the practice had gradually fallen out of use. Therefore there were many men who had not been knighted who were technically eligible. These could be summoned and fined for failing to show their support for the king. Charles was not interested in creating more knights and even those ineligible because they had been too young in 1626, or who were not in the highest level of society, were liable to be fined. By these means a total of about £170,000, the equivalent of three parliamentary subsidies, was raised by the end of the 1630s. Despite its success, distraint of knighthood carried a heavy cost. As Clarendon wrote 'though it had a foundation in right, yet, in the circumstances of proceedings, was very grievous and no less unjust'. Lord Montagu doubted that the king was wise to strain the loyalty of those fined for such short-term gain 'I find that many gentlemen that were forward in the loan [of 1626] ... troubled that no more respect is had of them than of those that refused'. Political loyalty in the past gave no protection against unfair demands and this strained men's allegiance.

It seemed unfair that men should be penalised for ignoring an obsolete custom, but no one doubted the legality of knighthood fines. The application of forest law was much more dubious. The boundaries of the royal forests were declared to be those of the time of Henry II, when they had reached their maximum extent. Suddenly large numbers of people found that they were technically living in a royal forest and could be fined for various offences such as engaging in agriculture. Rockingham Forest was enlarged from six to sixty square miles and the Earl of Salisbury was fined £20,000. Other landowners were fined up to £4,000 for enclosing land. This was considered a social evil because enclosing common land, usually for sheep which required little attention, could force small farmers and landless men who had previously been employed in the large open fields, into vagrancy. But as with most of the financial expedients of the Personal Rule, the intention was not to rectify an evil but to extract money, so the enclosures remained while the treasury was enriched.

Revenue from the court of wards was increased to a maximum of £83,000 in 1638-40 compared to a maximum of £35,000 in 1617-22. This was achieved by increasing wardship fines and by improved efficiency in the operation of the court. This financial gain to the crown was bought at considerable cost to the families unfortunate enough to be caught in wardship by the untimely death of the estate holder. The unpredictability and unfairness of many of the prerogative rights were in large part responsible for their unpopularity. Even if men escaped the worst exactions, they could see their neighbours being less fortunate and could fear for themselves in the future. Other methods of raising money were less important financially but caused considerable irritation to those affected. They included a proclamation against remaining in London without permission. The justification for this was that the gentry were needed in their localities to preserve order and to keep local government functioning efficiently. One man was fined £1,000 for ignoring the proclamation. Men could also be fined for building too near the capital and for eating meat in Lent.

What rankled in all these cases was the unfairness of the impositions and their arbitrary nature. They were seen as an attack on property, and they affected the political classes most severely. This was the very group whose support was vital to the king. Sir Arthur Haselrig described these years as a time when two or three gentlemen could not go out together without being charged with a riot. It was also seen as an abuse of the king's prerogative. The Earl of Clare who was charged in Star Chamber with both illegal building in London and depopulation, declared that proclamations were stretching the law and that the king was using his prerogative to extend his power. Another problem with such sources of finance was that they provided no permanent solution to the king's need for adequate supply. As the Venetian ambassador put it: 'All these may be called false mines for obtaining money, because they are good for once only and states are not maintained by such devices'.

d) Monopolies and Grants

Other means of raising money were more permanent but no less unpopular. Charles broke the spirit of the 1624 Statute of Monopolies by exploiting a loophole that enabled him to grant monopolies to companies rather than to individuals. These grants were bitterly resented as a crude form of purchase tax where most benefit went to the patentees. It has been estimated that for every £100,000 raised for the king, £750,000 went into the pockets of the patent holders. Clarendon was blunt: 'Projects of many kinds, many ridiculous, many scandalous, all very grievous, were set on foot; the envy and reproach of which came to the king, the profit to other men'. The soap monopoly was especially unpopular. Not only did prices rise but also the new company included a number of Catholics and it was claimed that the soap was of inferior quality. For the crown the 'popish soap' brought in £29,000 a year by 1636. Some measures were resented because private gain was put above the interests of the wider community. Grants of licences to export grain were especially unpopular and could provoke violence.

Office holders would often neglect their duties once they had secured their positions for life. Men won contracts either because the king wished to reward them for some service or because they were willing to pay for them. The blurring of patronage, revenue raising and law enforcement was upsetting to the notion of the king as a father to his people who would put their concerns first. The taint of money seemed to enter into every transaction, when ideas of loyalty, obedience and responsibility were more appropriate. The financial position of the crown was restored by the mid-1630s but the political cost had been high. Each new expedient brought a fresh wave of indignation which was revealed in the attacks on prerogative rights made in the Long Parliament, which swept them all away. The pettiness of most of the financial schemes did not justify their political cost. In 1636 the rejoicing on the death of the Attorney-General William Noy who had devised and defended many expedients for making money showed how annoying many of them were considered to be. Many people

1 now stick not to express a gladness that he is gone; and say (by way of irony) that now the project of soap will be washed and wiped away, that of buildings will fall, that of tobacco vanish into smoke, that of fuel be plucked up by the roots, that of victuals and
5 provisions be unprovided of a patron, that of taverns have the very memory of it drowned in cups of wine and that now gentlemen and their ladies (who were driven by him to the solitary life of the country) will be at liberty to return and reside in the city at their pleasure.

e) Ship Money

The most profitable of the new ways of raising money was ship money. This was a levy which was accepted as necessary in times of emergency for the defence of the seas. In 1634 it was levied on coastal counties because of the need to build up the fleet to guard against the depredations of pirates who regularly raided the south coast and carried young people into slavery. In 1635 it was levied again, but this time, against all precedent, it was extended to cover the whole country. Each year until 1640 the tax was demanded, which was unheard of, no matter that all the money received did go to the Treasury of the Navy and none to the ordinary expenditure of the government. The 'emergency' seemed to have become permanent and Charles to have introduced a national system of taxation by the back door. In 1638 a Somerset grand jury complained of 'the great and heavy taxations, by new invented ways upon the country'. The key word was 'new'. Like so much else that Charles's government was doing, ship money was innovatory and against tradition. Initially the tax was extremely successful. It raised £190,000 a year and the rate of non-payment was very low - 2.5 per cent in the first three years. However, the methods of assessing and collecting the tax gave rise to much opposition. Collection was the duty of the sheriff in each county who in turn relied on parish constables. The sheriff, who was the chief agent of royal authority in each of the shires, was made personally responsible for collecting the sum decided for his county and this placed a heavy burden on him, both financially and in terms of time. Some sheriffs were still trying to collect arrears and satisfy the Privy Council long after their terms of office were over. The unpleasantness of collecting the tax weakened support for the government among the gentry upon whom it was heavily dependent. In order to spread the burden of taxation and also to widen its scope, new ratings systems were introduced in many areas. In Essex in 1640 there were 3,200 on the roll for parliamentary subsidies, but 14,500 were assessed for ship money. This was much more equitable, but spreading the net of taxation wider meant more people were affected by it and this led to a greater degree of political awareness which would be significant when parliament reassembled. New rating systems also provided an easy target for those who opposed the tax and there were numerous appeals against the assessments, which impeded collection. The strain imposed upon unpaid local officials, principally the sheriff, was enormous and in the absence of parliamentary sanction, the resulting ill-feeling could only be directed at the regime. Nevertheless, despite the grumbles and dissatisfaction, up to 1637 ship money was the most profitable tax ever recorded in peace-time. In October 1637 John Burgh wrote his weekly dispatch to the ambassador in Paris:

1 I think that great tax of the ship money is so well digested (the honour of the business sinking now into apprehension and amongst most winning an affection to it) I suppose [it] will become perpetual ... time can season and form minds to comply with 5 public necessities.

This forecast was to prove hopelessly wrong. The following month John Hampden, a member of the Buckinghamshire gentry, was brought to trial for refusal to pay. Charles was keen to have the judges pronounce on ship money because it would strengthen his claim to collect it (remember the result of Bate's Case in 1606). The case aroused enormous interest nationally and when five of the twelve judges refused to find for the king, it was a moral victory for Hampden. In 1638 the amount collected fell by 20 per cent. Hampden's Case might have proved less significant if it had not coincided with the attempt to impose a new prayer book on the Scots. There was increased suspicion about what the money was intended for and, even more important, the level of government financial demands became excessive. By 1639, the king was also demanding money for the militia to fight the Scots and payment fell to 20 per cent. The provinces were being squeezed twice and there were fears of riots if ship money was pressed too far. Ship money could only be sustained when the local elites gave it their co-operation. Once that broke down, as men put the interests of their localities above that of the government, ship money collapsed as well.

6 Opposition

In 1637 there seemed scarcely a ripple on the calm surface of politics. One observer commented to a friend 'our times here are so quiet that they yield no occurrence worth the relation'. Another wrote

> All things are at this instant here in that calmness that there is very little of novelty to write ... for all business goes undisturbedly on in the strong current of the present time to which all men for the most part submit, and that effects this quietness.

Clarendon, who later fought for the king in the civil war and wrote a history of it in the 1660s, looked back on the 1630s as a time when the kingdom enjoyed

> the greatest calm and the fullest measure of felicity that any people in any age, for so long time together, have been blessed with, to the wonder and envy of all parts of Christendom.

The monarchy for the first time in decades was solvent. The country was at peace and there were no enemies posing a serious threat to security. The king was in excellent health and he had five children so there were no fears about the succession. It appeared that Charles could go on governing without a parliament and long usage would probably have resigned the majority to his most contentious reforms in the Church. This apparently rosy picture raises a number of questions. If everything was so splendid in 1637, why was the political nation united against Charles in 1640? Did the crisis of 1640 really spring from the events of 1637-40 or were there longer-term discontents?

It is on these two crucial questions that the revisionists part company with most of their fellow historians. The starting point of Conrad

Russell's book on *The Causes of the English Civil War* is 1637. The post-revisionist Ann Hughes in her book of the same title looks further back and identifies sources of conflict from the beginning of the century. If Charles's policies between 1637 and 1640 and his mishandling of the crises which resulted were not solely to blame for the united opposition he faced in the Long Parliament of 1640, what is the explanation for the lack of opposition in the 1630s?

In the absence of parliament which was the main forum for voicing political opposition, there was very little opportunity to express any disagreement with royal policies. To do so openly, for example in a pamphlet, invited charges of sedition or even treason and the fearful penalties these entailed. The fate of Prynne, Bastwick and Burton (see page 99), although an extreme example, aroused widespread revulsion. With such dire examples it is not surprising that there was little outward opposition to Charles's rule during the 1630s. People might dislike government policies but there was no effective way of combining to express that dislike. Significantly, there was an upsurge in emigration. In 1630, for example, 11 ships with a total of about 700 passengers left for the New World, many seeking the godly commonwealth they could not establish at home. A few of the most active Puritan opponents of the king joined together in the Providence Island Company, ostensibly to colonize the West Indian island of Providence but clearly its members, including John Pym, the Earl of Warwick, Lord Brooke and Lord Saye and Sele encouraged each other to maintain an opposition. For the rest, their dissatisfaction had to be expressed obliquely. By 1636, when it appeared that ship money had ceased to be an occasional emergency levy and had become an annual tax, disputes over assessments increased markedly in a way that reveals popular discontent. It is surely no coincidence that Tintinhull hundred, home of the prominent parliamentary critic Sir Robert Phelips, produced more rating disputes than any other hundred in the country. It was by such indirect means that people could indicate their unhappiness at events, but with such muted expression Charles could withdraw into the isolation of his court supremely indifferent or merely ignorant of the effect of his policies. A parliament would have warned the king about the depth of dissatisfaction in the country. As it was, he did not call one until he was so deeply committed to unpopular policies in Scotland that no easy retreat was possible - certainly not for Charles who was always convinced that he was right.

7 The Law

1 And here the damage and mischief cannot be expressed that the
Crown and State sustained by the deserved reproach and infamy
that attended the judges, by being made use of in this and like acts

of power; there being no possibility to preserve the dignity,
5 reverence and estimation of the laws themselves but by the
integrity and innocency of the judges ... If these men had preserved
the simplicity of their ancestors in severely and strictly defending
the laws, other men had observed the modesty of theirs in humbly
and dutifully obeying them.
    Clarendon, *History of the Rebellion 1646-67*

1 Acts of Parliament to take away [the king's] royal power in the
defence of his kingdom are void ... They are void acts of parliament
to bind the king not to command the subjects' persons and goods,
and I say their money too, for, no Acts of Parliament make any
5 difference.
    Sir John Finch, Lord Chief Justice - Judgement in Hampden's
    Case 1638

1 Where Mr Holborne [Hampden's counsel] supposed a fundamental policy ... that in case the monarch of England should be inclined
to exact from his subjects at his pleasure he should be restrained,
for that he could have nothing from them, but upon a common
5 consent of parliament. He is utterly mistaken herein ... The law
knows no such king-yoking policy. The law is of itself an old and
trusty servant of the king's ... There are two maxims of the law of
England ... The first is "that the king is a person trusted with the
state of the commonwealth". The second of these maxims is "that
10 the king can do no wrong".
    Sir Robert Berkeley - Judgement in Hampden's Case 1638

One of parliament's functions was not only to make the law but also
to interpret it in its role as the highest court in the land. In its
absence the lower courts assumed a greater significance either as the
bastion of tradition against the encroaching power of the monarchy
or as the supporter of royal authority. Hampden's case illustrates this
contradiction. The question was whether the king was the ultimate
source of power able to raise ship money by declaring that an
emergency existed because of the presence of pirates, or whether the
common law gave protection against arbitrary demands without
parliamentary sanction. On one hand, the views of Berkeley and
Finch gave additional credibility to Charles's policies, although their
use for justifying a policy like ship money called them into question
as Clarendon indicates. On the other hand, and more surprisingly,
five judges gave contrary judgements despite the knowledge that
Charles was prepared to remove those who disagreed with him. Sir
Ranulph Crewe was dismissed as Chief Justice of the King's Bench
for refusing to validate the forced loan in 1627. Sir George Croke
stated that ship money was against 'divers statutes' and that

1 no pretence of prerogative, royal power, necessity or danger, doth
  or can make it good ... The common law of England sets a freedom
  in the subjects in respect of their persons, and gives them a true
  property in their goods and estates, so that without their consent -
5 that is to say their private, actual consent, or (implicitly) in
  parliament - it cannot be taken from them.

Croke's judgement was in direct contradiction to that of Sir John Finch
and illustrated the uncertainty of relying on the common law to buttress
a particular policy. The prerogative courts of Star Chamber and High
Commission were much more reliable politically. Star Chamber was an
ad hoc body made up of members of the Privy Council. It was used to
attack those who disagreed with government policy. It was particularly
useful as a means of raising revenue because it was speedy and efficient
in its dealings and it was able to impose huge fines. These were seldom
collected in full, but negotiations to get them reduced could drag on for
years and enormous resentment was generated amongst those, like the
Earl of Clare, who were called before the court.

Sir Edward Coke described Star Chamber as 'the most honourable
court (our Parliament excepted) that is in the Christian world'. By 1640
justice seemed to take second place to money. Pym was able to say 'the
Star Chamber now is become a court of revenue'. The provision of
justice was one of the monarch's most important functions. Allowing the
courts to be debased into mere collectors of money did much to
undermine trust in Charles's government. Star Chamber also lost
respect because Archbishop Laud used it to enforce his extremely
unpopular reforms in the Church. Prynne, Burton and Bastwick's trial
was the most notorious of numerous proceedings against those who had
challenged the Archbishop's ideas. The severity of their sentence was
unusual, but it had an enormous effect. This was the case not so much
for the ideas which they expressed (they had been punished for these
before without comment) but the nature of the punishment itself and
the degradation of three gentlemen. Arbitrary government seemed to be
growing. Star Chamber was seen as an agent of despotism even though
most of its business was non-political and even trivial. One case which
had more serious repercussions for the crown than most was the trial of
the City of London in 1635 over its failure to populate the plantation of
Londonderry. The City lost its Irish lands, incurred a fine of £70,000
(later reduced) and was publicly humiliated. The City had previously
been one of the king's most fervent supporters. He promoted trade and
could dispense valuable patronage in the form of customs farms or
monopolies. In return, the City was the first place to which the king
would look when he wanted a generous loan. It is a measure of Charles's
ineptitude to have so alienated the City that when he asked for a loan to
fight the Scots in 1639 they first granted him a paltry £5000 and
thereafter refused any more support.

8 Ireland

The most troublesome of Charles's three kingdoms was Ireland. This Catholic country had had an alien Protestant ruling class imposed upon it and then, in the wake of the rebellion at the start of the century, a series of plantations were created. Land was taken from its original holders if they could not prove a valid title to it and was given to Protestant settlers. This policy affected not only the native Irish but also the Catholic 'Old English' who had lived in Ireland for centuries. Charles used their insecurity to extract money for his wars in the 1620s by promising to make concessions known as 'the Graces' which confirmed their right to hold land. These Graces were not confirmed and their implementation became a major objective of the Catholics.

In 1632 Ireland was a financial liability to England. There was an annual deficit of £20,000. It was at this point that Sir Thomas Wentworth was appointed Lord Deputy of Ireland. He had been a prime mover in the Petition of Right but then he had accepted the offer of royal service and had become Lord President of the Council of the North. Wentworth was one of the most energetic and efficient members of the Privy Council which is probably why Charles never liked him or admitted him to his inner circle of advisers. Sending him to Ireland was a good way of securing Wentworth's services while keeping him distant from the real sources of power. Wentworth had a genius for alienating people and was arrogant and insensitive. His one ally at court was William Laud. Together they conceived a style of government known as 'Thorough'. This elevated the king's prerogative and placed great emphasis on central authority and close supervision of local officers. It also sought to make government more efficient and less corrupt. Those who opposed this style of government they characterised in their letters to each other as 'Mona Lott'. The attempt to develop 'Thorough' as a method of government in England had very limited success, but in Ireland, Wentworth was able to impose much stricter control and to achieve apparent acquiescence to royal commands. Although Wentworth was absent from court for the whole of the 1630s, he came to symbolise the hated aspects of the Personal Rule because of his time in Ireland.

Wentworth brought the Irish Parliament into a position of subservience by exerting great pressure in the choice of parliamentary candidates and by refusing to allow any debate until the crown's financial needs had been dealt with. He skilfully exploited the divisions in Irish society to gain more money. For example, in 1634 he promised to implement the Graces in return for additional subsidies from parliament. Then he broke his word and forged an alliance with the Protestant 'New English'. This was short-lived because of Wentworth's Arminian religious policy and a campaign to win back Church lands. Initially Wentworth was very successful in Ireland. He ended the deficit and Ireland began to contribute to the English treasury. He extended the powers of the prerogative courts and claimed royal title to huge tracts of land. Large fines were imposed on those who opposed his measures. The administration of customs was made more efficient and smuggling was attacked. In the Church, Laudians were appointed against the wishes of the Puritan Archbishop Ussher. Together these policies brought in increased revenue, a more efficient administration and a reformed church. But it was bought at enormous cost. He alienated every section of society so that within two years of his departure royal authority had collapsed as rebellion swept the country. In England his policies had been watched with foreboding as his opponents brought their complaints to the Privy Council in an unsuccessful attempt to get Wentworth's actions reversed. He returned from Ireland at the end of 1639, summoned by an anxious king; 'Come when you will. Ye shall be welcome to your assured friend'. The problem now lay in how to handle the Scots.

9 Scotland

Charles had been born in Scotland but showed little enthusiasm for his birthplace. He made one visit in 1618 after arriving in England and it took him eight years to go to Edinburgh for his coronation in 1633. Then he stayed for only two weeks. In an era of personal monarchy it was important to see the king regularly because he was the source of patronage and power. All monarchs experienced problems in ruling multiple kingdoms unless they went out of their way to ensure that all parts of their dominions received equal attention. In practice this was difficult to achieve and it was not only Charles I who encountered opposition. The Spanish king's problems were even worse with revolts in Catalonia and Portugal in mid-century. The Scots felt slighted by Charles's neglect of them and they had some justification for bitterness towards England. Scotland was much poorer, she was economically backward in comparison with her southern neighbour, and her institutions were accorded less prestige than their English counterparts. The Scottish Privy Council had nine non-resident English members whereas the English Privy Council had only four or five Scots. It was the English who received the bulk of royal patronage and the Scots were excluded from England's growing overseas trade. In 1625, without warning or explanation, Charles's first act with regard to Scotland had been to revoke all grants of land made by the crown since 1540. This included the church and monastic lands given to the nobility as a result of the Reformation. It affected almost all families of substance and was an extraordinarily tactless move. Two years later this was changed so that men could retain their lands on crown leases, the income going to subsidise the stipends of church ministers. This was a generally successful scheme but, like so much else that Charles did, the political price was very high. The nobility, already excluded from power, felt alienated from the crown. However, opposition remained passive while the nobility was at odds with the Presbyterian ministers who exerted great influence on political life. Charles was so inept that he united these two strands into a fervent nationalist uprising by a heavy-handed attempt to introduce a new prayer book.

It was a source of disquiet to both Charles and Laud that there was not uniformity of religion in the three kingdoms. Scotland was unusual in having a national religious settlement supported by the vast majority of the population which had become unacceptable to its sovereign. Charles knew that if he was to get the English prayer book accepted in Scotland he would have to proceed with tact and understanding. So, before he introduced the new prayer book, he carefully consulted the bishops and made a number of changes to render the book more acceptable to the Scots. For example, the word 'priest' was deleted. But the bishops were not really representative of the Scots and the Scottish nobles at court, such as the Marquess of Hamilton, were very anglicised.

The biggest mistake came in the manner of the prayer book's imposition. It was not shown to the Scottish Parliament or Church Assembly but was introduced by royal proclamation, abandoning all pretence of government by consent. When the new prayer book was used at St Giles' Cathedral, Edinburgh, in July 1637 there was a riot. The woman who called out 'the mass is entered upon us!' expressed the opinion of nine-tenths of the Scottish people. Protestantism and patriotism combined in a powerful mood of resistance. Charles ignored the frantic warnings from his Scottish ministers about the gravity of the situation and believed that firmness would end the problem, a view shared by Laud who advised the king to 'risk everything rather than yield a jot'. In February 1638 Charles brought matters to a head by issuing a proclamation making protests against the new prayer book an act of treason. The Scots now had to choose between loyalty to the king and loyalty to the Presbyterian Church. A document called the 'Covenant' was drawn up to which hundreds of thousands of Scots subscribed, swearing to resist to the death the innovations in religion. Charles refused to back down. He sent the Marquess of Hamilton to negotiate but had no intention of making any concessions and both sides began making military preparations.

1 I expect not anything can reduce that people to obedience but force only ... In the meantime your care must be to dissolve the multitude, and (if it be possible), to possess yourselves in Edinburgh and Stirling (which I do not expect), and, to this end I
5 give you leave to flatter them.
   Charles to Hamilton June 1638

1 The great and considerable forces lately raised in Scotland,
without order or warrant from us, by the instigation of some
factious persons ill affected to monarchical government, who seek
to cloak their too apparent rebellious designs under pretence of
5 religion, albeit we have often given them good assurance of our
resolution constantly to maintain the religion established by the
laws of that kingdom, have moved us to take into our royal care to
provide for the preservation and safety of this our kingdom of
England, which is by the tumultuous proceedings of those factious
10 spirits in apparent danger to be annoyed and invaded.

Charles to the Earl of Suffolk, February 1639.

10 The Bishops' War

To gain time Charles agreed to summon a Scottish general assembly to
meet in November. This abolished episcopacy, and Charles resolved to
suppress the rebels, as he saw them, by force. Contrary to all precedent,
he did not call a parliament. Instead, he summoned the peers to meet
him at York in April 1639 with appropriate assistance. This brought to a
head a number of issues which had been simmering just below the
surface. Many already felt they were contributing excessively to the
exchequer and a tax strike began. People were uneasy about supporting
the king in his attempt to impose on the Scots Arminian practices which
were closely allied to Roman Catholicism in the popular mind.
However, the peers agreed to the king's demands with some reluctance,
but the quality of the troops assembled at Berwick was so appalling that
a campaign against the Scots could not be contemplated. The two sides
reached agreement in the Treaty of Berwick in June 1639. A Scottish
parliament was to meet and both sides would demobilise.

The relief which greeted this agreement was short-lived. To Charles's
delight, the parliament was dissolved without achieving anything. 'They
must not imagine that our granting of a free assembly and parliament
obliges us to ratify all their fancies'. Wentworth was recalled from
Ireland and was finally given the earldom that he craved. The new Earl
of Strafford urged the king to call a parliament, judging from his
experience in Ireland that it would be easy to handle. The rest of the
Privy Council were not so sure, but Charles agreed to meet another
parliament in April 1640 in the hope that it would grant him sufficient
money to crush the Scots.

11 The Short Parliament

There had been periodic calls for a parliament throughout the 1630s but
people greeted the news that another parliament had been summoned
with some caution. They were not convinced that the king intended to

restore a working relationship with parliament. By not calling one earlier Charles had lost the opportunity to unite the country behind him in his campaign against the Scots. It was traditional to summon a parliament at the outset of a war, not only to get subsidies but also for propaganda purposes so that the nation could join together against the enemy. One of the functions of parliament was to give legitimacy to royal acts. But this was not its only role, and in the absence of parliament for eleven years there might be other matters more pressing than supporting the king's war. There were many issues in the 1630s which had promoted division - ship money, changes in religion, and the activities of the prerogative courts - and these would need discussion. There was an accumulation of grievances which would require careful handling by the king if he wished parliament to be generous. The elections aroused an unprecedented degree of interest. The concerns of the Lincolnshire electorate were encapsulated in the rhyme:

> Choose no ship sheriff, nor court atheist
> No fen drainer, nor church papist.

The king's hope of a quick and profitable session of parliament was not to be realised. Lord Keeper Finch ended his opening speech with the warning that 'the king did not require their advice, but an immediate vote of supplies'. Unmoved, the Commons began to discuss their grievances which were put by John Pym in a famous speech into three categories: infringement of parliamentary liberties, innovations in religion, and violations of property. The Commons were not prepared to make any new grant of money until the question of ship money had been settled. Charles offered to relinquish ship money in return for twelve subsidies but before the Commons had had any real chance to discuss the matter, the king dissolved parliament after only three weeks. He did so probably because he had unrealistic expectations of the speed at which an occasional legislative body with no effective leadership could be expected to take decisions; but his impatience filled the country with foreboding.

Charles had lost an opportunity to swing the country behind him. Now his position was far worse. Parliament had not voted any money, only a small minority was still paying ship money, there were demonstrations of discontent in London, and reports of unrest in the country. Some Members of Parliament were questioned and imprisoned. The crown seemed to be acting in an increasingly autocratic manner.

The levies raised to fight the Scots were threatening to mutiny across the country. In July 1640 the Scots invaded Northumberland. This came as a relief to many people because it gave them a lever to put pressure on the king. Since there was no royal army capable of meeting the Scots, Charles had to agree to a truce at Ripon in October. The Scots were allowed to occupy Northumberland and County Durham and were paid a subsidy of £850 a day until peace could be made. This effectively tied Charles's hands. He had to summon a parliament to get money to pay the Scots and he would not be able to dismiss it while the Scots remained in England. This removed the king's principal weapon against a difficult parliament - that he could dissolve it at will. This parliament would not be like the one in the spring. The political nation was united in its determination to remedy the ills of the past eleven years and to return to the traditional government of England. In their search for that tradition, and a means of enforcing it on the king, they were to be drawn ever deeper into radicalism until the very throne itself was abolished. But that was far in the future, undreamt of by any on the day, as John Evelyn saw it, 'that long, ungrateful, foolish and fatal parliament opened' on 4 November 1640.

12 Conclusion

The personal rule is no longer seen as the 'Eleven Years' Tyranny' but there is a broad consensus that Charles I made serious mistakes in his handling of the country which led to the uniting of virtually the entire political nation against him. Where historians do disagree is in how they allocate responsibility for the breakdown in relations. The current orthodoxy is that of revisionism. This puts some of the blame on the House of Commons for failing to provide adequate finance for Charles to govern effectively, especially in the context of a war. This related to a long-term problem with crown finances. There had been a steady erosion in the value of royal revenues since about the 1580s. This was not fully understood at the time and the increased demands upon parliament for additional revenue caused strains in the relationship with the king. There were no serious issues of principle driving Charles and parliament apart except in religion and in the perception that Charles was trying to introduce Catholicism by the back door. Charles abandoned parliamentary government largely as a matter of expediency because to gain anything he had to make too many concessions. The civil war did not become inevitable until 1642 and was the result of unfortunate choices by Charles (such as the imposition of the prayer book in Scotland) and a series of coincidences.

The post-revisionists have sought to modify this analysis. They argue that there were fundamental differences between those who believed in the divine right of kings and those who thought that the constitution rested on tradition and the common law. In general, they regard Charles I less favourably than the revisionists (who themselves were reacting against the pro-parliamentary analysis of the Whigs and Marxists). The British dimension of Scotland and Ireland is seen as crucial for events in England. Charles is criticised for failing to take note of 'country' concerns. This came to mean a desire for parliamentary government, a Calvinist Church of England and a king who did not cut himself off in an enclosed and alien court. The biggest mistake Charles made during the personal rule was undoubtedly the decision to persist with the Scottish prayer book even after the ferocity of the opposition had become apparent. The handling of the Scots showed Charles at his worst - obstinate, deceitful and untrustworthy. Up to 1637, the decision to rule without parliament had worked well for him. There was less tiresome opposition to take notice of and the country was enjoying a period of peace and prosperity while much of continental Europe was ravaged by war. Could it have been sustained indefinitely? It is impossible to be certain on this point, but, with the bulk of crown revenue now coming from the customs, there was no immediate threat to the continuance of non-parliamentary rule. If Charles had concentrated on securing his position and had heeded warnings about his policies which were unpopular, he might never have had to face another parliament. Unfortunately, it was in Charles's nature to press ahead with anything that he considered right, regardless of the consequences. It is such people who become martyrs.

Making notes on *'The Personal Rule of Charles I, 1629-40'*

This chapter covers a period which in many ways was the culmination of all that had gone before. It was during the 1630s that Charles I pursued the policies which were to lead to his downfall. There were no parliaments to provide a distraction or an impression that the crown was being unfairly criticised. The Duke of Buckingham was dead and no one else assumed such a powerful position, so policies were seen to be the king's responsibility. It is your task to understand what policies Charles followed and how they affected opinion in the country. You should be able to explain the extent and nature of opposition to the crown and what had caused it. Use the following headings and questions as a framework for your notes.

1 Charles and Parliament   Summarise briefly, and in your own words, what had gone wrong since 1625 between Charles and parliament
1.1 The Role of Parliament
    Make sure you can explain parliament's role in the government of the country. What difference did it make if parliament did not meet?
2 Charles's Government
    How would you characterise the government of the 1630s?
    Can it be seen in any way as a tyranny?
3 The Court
    What was Charles's court like? Why did it arouse suspicion?
4 Rule without Parliament
    List the problems facing the government in 1629
5 Finance Describe briefly the crown's major sources of revenue and how they were exploited to give more money a) Customs
    b) Economies c) Prerogative Rights d) Monopolies and grants

5.1 Ship Money Why was it so unpopular?
6. Opposition
    What mechanisms were there for the expression of opposition? Why
    was there so little outward opposition to Charles's policies?
7 The Law What part did the courts play in the personal rule?
8 Ireland What was the nature of Wentworth's rule in Ireland?
9 Scotland What mistakes were made in the government of Scotland?
10 The Bishops' War
11 The Short Parliament

Answering essay questions on 'The Personal Rule of Charles I,
1629-40'

1 How much justification had Charles I for ruling without
   parliament from 1629 to 1640, and for the methods he used to
   raise money in these years?
2 'Charles I's attempt to rule without parliament from 1629 to
   1640 was a serious mistake'. Discuss.
3 'She enjoyed the greatest calm and the fullest measure of felicity
   that any country has been blessed with.' Do you agree with this
   view of England during the personal rule of Charles I?
4 Assess whether the outcome of the ship money case hastened the
   end of the personal rule.
5 Was Charles I's attachment to Arminianism the main cause of
   the increasing dissatisfaction with his personal rule?
6 What circumstances led to the Petition of Right in 1628? Did it
   accomplish anything or have any meaning over the next twelve
   years?
7 Why was Charles I unable to solve the problems of governing the
   country in the period 1625-40?

Some of these questions cover a wide range of material, such as question
7, others are more limited in their scope, such as question 4. These
questions present opposite problems. In the first there seems to be too
much to deal with in a 45 minute essay. In the second there may be a
danger of running out of things to say unless you are thoroughly
prepared on that topic. When a big subject is undertaken it is important
not to begin in a narrative or descriptive manner. In question 7 it would
be impossible to give a complete account of the reign of Charles from
1625 to 1640 and this is not what the examiner wants. These broad
questions require careful organisation of your material and a limited
selection of facts. The important thing is your argument. Decide what
the main issues were and then consider how best to illustrate them.
   For question 7 you should bear in mind relations with parliament -
why these broke down; finance and the lack of it; and religion, and the
drive to uniformity. You should also consider whether Charles was such
a failure as the question implies. If you restrict yourself to one paragraph

for each subject you will find that you are automatically selecting what to include and what to leave out. A useful tip is to think how you would answer the question verbally to a non-historian friend and that will concentrate your mind on the important issues.

Questions of apparently limited scope often have hidden implications. Question 4 is relatively straightforward. As well as looking at ship money and the effects of the case, you must examine the other reasons why the personal rule came to an end - principally Charles's policy in Scotland. Although you must consider whether a question has additional implications, it is true that some cover more ground than others and in the more limited questions it is of greater importance that you do not omit matters of significance.

Source-based questions on 'The Personal Rule of Charles I, 1629-40'

1 Contarini on Parliament
Carefully read the account by the Venetian ambassador, Contarini, on the dissolution of parliament in 1629, given on pages 110-11. Answer the following questions.
a) What were the two issues identified by Contarini which were driving the king and parliament apart? (2 marks)
b) Does Contarini see the king or parliament as being more successful in their conflicts? Would this view have been shared by a member of the Commons? (5 marks)
c) What do you think Contarini meant by the phrase 'to lose his crown'? (3 marks)

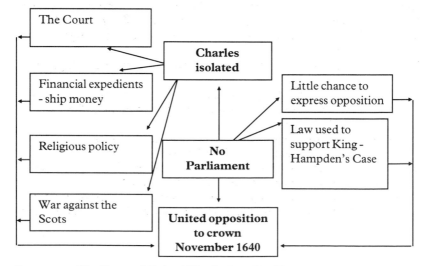

Summary - The Personal Rule of Charles I, 1629-40

2 The Ship Money Case
Carefully read Clarendon and the three extracts from the judgement in
Hampden's case, given on pages 125-7. Answer the following questions.
a) Explain in your own words the judgement of Sir John Finch.
   (3 marks)
b) Explain in your own words the judgement of Sir Robert Berkeley.
   (5 marks)
c) Explain in your own words the judgement of Sir George Croke. How
   did this justify the refusal to pay ship money? (5 marks)
d) What is Clarendon's complaint against the judges? (3 marks)
e) Is this a valid criticism of the judges' actions and reasoning?
   (4 marks)

3 Charles and Scotland
Carefully read the extracts from Charles's letters to the Marquess of
Hamilton and the Earl of Suffolk, given on pages 130-1. Answer the
following questions.
a) What do the two extracts tell us about Charles and his attitude
   to i) negotiations, and ii) the grievances of the Scots? (4 marks)
b) What reasons did the Scots have for doubting that Charles would
   'maintain the religion established by the laws of that kingdom'?
   (3 marks)
c) Was Charles right in the motives for fighting that he attributed to the
   Scots in his letter to Suffolk? Explain your answer. (3 marks)

4 The Political Implications of Art
Carefully study the etching by Wenceslaus Hollar of Whitehall Palace
showing Inigo Jones's Banqueting Hall on page 117, and the picture of
Charles I with his family on page 115. Answer the following questions.
a) Describe how the Banqueting Hall differs from the buildings around
   it. (3 marks)
b) Explain why it was regarded with disfavour by many English people.
   (3 marks)
c) In the background of the painting of Charles and his family there is
   the Parliament House. What is much more prominent in front of it
   on the table? (2 marks)
d) What does this arrangement suggest the painting was trying to
   convey about the balance of political power? (3 marks)
e) Why might pictures showing Charles I as a devoted family man have
   been a cause for concern in the country? (2 marks)
f) Charles I was the first English king to have been painted frequently
   with his family. Can you suggest why this should have been the case?
   (2 marks)

CHAPTER 8

Conclusion

1 Historical Perspectives

In 1640 the political nation was united against Charles I and a serious crisis threatened to disrupt the working of the country's constitution which was based on mutual trust and understanding between the component parts of king, parliament and the judges. The events of the preceding 40 years and especially since 1629 had progressively eroded the sense that all parts of the machinery of government were working towards the same ends. Breakdown, in the form of civil war, was to overtake the constitution within two years but in November 1640 this was unsuspected by everyone. Major questions which should be considered are 'How far was the civil war inevitable by 1640?' and 'How successful was the rule of Charles up to 1640?'

The answers given to these questions reflect the personal beliefs of the historian. Whig historians of the eighteenth and nineteenth centuries saw events moving inexorably towards a conflict between king and parliament as the latter learnt to use its powers to extract concessions from the monarch and sought a more active role in government. In this analysis, the part played by Charles I hastened the arrival of war but was not the major determining factor. The Whigs saw him as an autocratic ruler attempting to undermine the property rights and liberties of his subjects - a view summed up by the description of the personal rule as the 'eleven years' tyranny'. The House of Commons, by contrast, was seen as the defender of liberty, the rule of law, and Protestantism.

The Marxist interpretation also sees a civil war as being inevitable by 1640, although for rather different reasons. This analysis puts more emphasis on economic developments and class conflict. The civil war is seen as a revolution by which the middle classes freed themselves from the restraints of a feudal society. Charles is regarded as blameworthy for impeding the growth of a capitalist class by trying to minimise the effects of social change, for example by issuing proclamations against enclosures. Both of these 'progressive' interpretations (the Whig and the Marxist) have become unfashionable since the 1960s.

In recent decades the civil war has come to be seen as a consequence of short-term causes acting on structural weaknesses in the system of government. At the same time Charles I has usually, although not invariably, been seen in a more favourable light. In clashes with parliament the House of Commons has been regarded as the innovator making demands that the king was bound to reject. It has been argued that it was only in religion that Charles departed from precedent by seeking to change the practice and belief of the Church of England in the face of strong opposition. These 'revisionist' accounts have tended to focus on the underlying weakness of the system of government caused by inflation and a shrinking revenue which made the king's task much more difficult, and to stress how important individual actions were in bringing about a breakdown of trust and the growth of conflict.

It can therefore be seen that there is no single correct answer to either of the two questions posed. Every historian will have his or her own interpretation which will be subtly or glaringly different from other people's. For most of us, situations such as this provide an important part of the fascination of the study of history. Anybody who can make a case for something and can properly back it up with an argument based on evidence has an interpretation that is as worthy of consideration as any other. It is in this light that the following analysis of Charles I's reign is offered. Once you have read it, a useful exercise would be to try to write your own interpretation of Charles from a strongly parliamentary perspective. You will find a royalist point of view later in the chapter.

2 One Possible Interpretation

In 1640 no one was contemplating a war against the king although tensions did exist. There were serious weaknesses in the structure of the government, above all the inability of the crown to live off revenues which the country accepted. This forced the king to obtain money from sources without parliamentary consent, most importantly from customs and later by means of ship money. Inevitably, this created problems when parliament met and increasingly distrust grew between king and the Commons, souring the political atmosphere. This led to a vicious circle where the apprehensions of each side were confirmed by the seemingly unreasonable behaviour of the other. So, at the start of the reign, Charles I could not understand why the Commons would not vote sufficient funds for the war against Spain which it had urged on the government. On the other hand, MPs wanted a clear declaration of intent from the crown about the defence of Protestantism and the nature of the war to be fought.

The second major cause of tension was religious division. To much of the country it did not seem that Charles was defending Protestantism. With his Catholic wife and his imposition of new ritual and ceremony there were fears that England was to return to Catholicism. These religious tensions were not new - they had been present in one form or another since the Reformation - but the deliberate Arminian campaign of Charles and Laud was seen as an attack on the central beliefs of the Church.

Religious division and structural weakness were not in themselves sufficient to cause a civil war, otherwise one would have broken out at any time from the later stages of Elizabeth's reign. The crucial additional factor in mid-century was the character of Charles I. He transformed the crisis of 1640 into a civil war but, perhaps more importantly, it was his policies which created the crisis of 1640. As we have seen, Charles was not a natural politician. He was unable to negotiate and compromise. He would listen to advice but once his mind was made up he was inflexible and convinced that his position was right. These qualities could have made for a perfectly successful ruler. Charles's misfortune was that he tended to pursue policies which were unpopular with many of his subjects. Nowhere was this clearer than in the field of religion. By the end of the 1630s a large proportion of the English feared for the existence of their Church. The disastrous attempt to impose similar changes on Scotland set in motion events which were to lead to war.

Scotland had its own system of government and separate institutions. It was the Kirk that was probably the most distinctive of these. Charles's heavy-handed attempt to alter the Kirk without consultation led his Scottish subjects to take up arms against him. Scotland already felt neglected by the king. One two-week visit in 1633 was no compensation for the feeling that England always came first and that it was English advice that was listened to. This did not encourage the Scots to put much faith in negotiating and they were quicker to resort to force than might have been the case if they had felt their grievances would receive a sympathetic hearing. The defeat of the English at Newburn weakened Charles and made him dependent for a settlement on parliament. This decisively altered the balance of power between them because the king could no longer dissolve the session when he chose. There was a serious crisis but war in England was still a long way off. So the answer to the first question is that war was not inevitable by 1640, but that Charles's religious policy and especially the fiasco over the Scottish prayer book had made it much more likely.

3 Criteria for Assessment

There are different ways of assessing success or failure. It is possible to think that an individual has been a great success because of their achievements while that same person believes themselves to be a failure because they could not achieve the one thing that was most important to them. Sir Edward Coke, celebrated for his defence of the common law, was disappointed never to be Lord Chancellor. Therefore, the first criterion might be to judge someone by his or her own aspirations. Secondly, one could assess the results of an individual's actions both in their immediate effect and in the long term. A good example of the way in which short and long-term effects can be very different is found in the protracted wars fought by Spain and France in the sixteenth and seventeenth centuries. Wars which initially brought great prestige ended up severely weakening the economies of both countries, especially Spain. A final way of judging performance is to look at actions in the light of the values and beliefs of the time or of the present day. We condemn Elizabeth I for executing Catholics and praise James I for being more tolerant. Contemporaries found nothing strange in religious persecution and most supported the policy against Catholics.

In addition to these different criteria for judging success which may produce very varied assessments of the same person, one can consider different parts of their achievements. A comprehensive look at Charles I would include relations with parliament, religion, foreign policy, Scotland and Ireland, the court and its culture and the king's ability to inspire loyalty and trust. Most historians will inevitably concentrate on one part of the picture rather than another and this often accounts for the diversity of opinions which can be held about an individual. Thus you can see that any measure of success or failure needs to be looked at carefully. Has the whole story been considered? Would an alternative perspective be as convincing? The following section does not attempt a balanced view - just the reverse! It is an examination of Charles I's reign as he might have seen it. There is no account taken of the legitimate grievances of others. It is intended to be provocative, to sting you into disagreement and to make you assess what you really do think about Charles and to decide by what criteria it would be most reasonable to judge him. How far were mistakes of his own making or were others also to blame?

4 The Rule of Charles I to 1640 - Success or Failure?

Charles I came to the throne in 1625 when England was on the brink of war with Spain. The new king had enjoyed harmonious relations with the parliament which was in session when James I died and there was apparent agreement on the subject of war and the need for adequate parliamentary finance. However, within only a few weeks, the House of Commons was behaving in an irresponsible and unreasonable manner. It refused to make the customary grant of tonnage and poundage to the king for life and it raised many objections about the war, some of them to do with tactics which was no business of theirs. In addition, the Commons questioned the right of the king to appoint his own ministers by objecting to the Duke of Buckingham whom they later tried to impeach. The king's marriage also caused trouble. Parliament disliked Charles marrying a Catholic but it had no grasp of political reality. He had to marry someone of equal status, preferably a princess with a sizeable dowry. Unfortunately there were no suitable Protestant candidates, which left France and Spain as the most appropriate choices. The Spanish were not interested and so the choice fell on Louis XIII's sister. Some concessions to the Catholics had to be made during the negotiations, but these were short-lived and Henrietta Maria presented no threat to the Church of England.

The foreign policy of the 1620s was not a success. However, parliament deserves most of the blame for this because it refused to provide sufficient finance. When the king was driven to raise money by other means such as the forced loan, it became even less co-operative and wasted its time drawing up the Petition of Right. If the Commons had met its obligations the efforts of Buckingham would not have been in vain and England would have had some military successes to glory in. Unfortunately, the Commons did not realise that only by working with the king rather than against him would anything be achieved and so he decided to rule alone.

In religion it was necessary to restore a sense of order and worship. Many churches had become too casual about maintaining a proper reverence and it was felt that a new ceremonialism would increase respect. There was some resistance to the reforms introduced by Laud, but this came mainly from those who encouraged an unhealthy reliance on individual conscience rather than trusting in the leaders whom God had appointed. These Puritans put too much emphasis on doctrine and not enough on conformity to the established Church. However, despite their opposition, the church reforms were going well by 1640 and they would soon have been accepted by the whole country.

The 1630s was a decade of peace and prosperity when most of the rest of Europe was involved in war. Charles made peace and he remained neutral throughout the 1630s despite negotiations with both Spain and France for an alliance. This left him free to concentrate on domestic matters. The inadequacy of the navy was remedied by the levying of ship money which provided funds for a new fleet. Local government was more closely supervised through the watchfulness of the Privy Council and such measures as the Book of Orders. Customs revenue soared, and all was tranquil.

This peace was shattered by the Scots rebels. They objected to an attempt to bring their worship into conformity with that in England. They mistakenly claimed that the new prayerbook was full of popish practices and they refused to negotiate in a reasonable way or to accept royal assurances that their faith was not in danger. The resort to arms weakened Charles's position. Although his financial position had greatly improved in the years without a parliament, it was still not strong enough to fight a war without additional funds which only the House of Commons could provide. This led to the summoning of parliament which, instead of dealing with the national emergency, began indulging in petty disputes over liberties and grievances. The success of the period without parliament shows that it was parliament which was responsible for the failures of Charles's reign. If his subjects had trusted the king more and been less ready to take up arms tragedy would not have occurred.

Working on the 'Conclusion'

There is no need to make detailed notes from this chapter. You should already have a comprehensive set of notes and now you should feel comfortable about the period and ready to answer the wider questions which can be asked about the early seventeenth century. What do you think about James I and Charles I? What part did parliament play in promoting discord in the first four decades of the century? Which historians do you find convincing? Make sure you can back up your answers with evidence. Carefully read through the conclusion again. Try to find areas where your analysis differs from the one that is given. This is something you may not feel ready to tackle until your studies are nearing their completion. It is much easier to accept what you read than to question the assumptions that lie behind it.

Chronological Table

1603   24 March, Elizabeth I died having nominated James VI of Scotland to succeed her. Robert Cecil retained as chief minister.

April, the Puritan Millenary Petition presented to James on his journey south.

1604   January, the Hampton Court Conference.

March, First Parliament opened, dispute over election returns, the Commons drew up the Apology.

August, Treaty of London ended war with Spain.

1605   November, the Gunpowder Plot.

1606-7   Third session of parliament, discussions on union. Bate's case confirmed the validity of impositions.

1608   New book of rates issued covering wide range of imports. Crown in severe financial difficulties.

Calvin's case: Scots born after 1603 were in effect naturalised English.

1610   Last session of the first parliament, the Great Contract. Its failure led to Cecil's disgrace.

1612-16 Robert Carr chief favourite at court.

1612   Henry, Prince of Wales died. Prince Charles now heir.

1613   Princess Elizabeth married Frederick V of the Palatinate.

1614-23 Sporadic negotiations with Spain over match between Charles and Spanish Infanta.

1614   Addled Parliament.

1614-18 Corrupt Earl of Suffolk was Lord Treasurer.

1615   Cockayne's Scheme.

1616   Buckingham became chief favourite.

1618   Thirty Years War began.

1619   Frederick takes the throne of Bohemia.

1621   Third Parliament met. Discussed foreign policy and monopolies. Lord Chancellor Bacon was impeached. Fearing for their privileges, the Commons entered the Protestation in their journal.

1621-4   Cranfield was Lord Treasurer.

1623   Trip to Madrid by Charles and Buckingham who became a duke in his absence.

1624   Fourth Parliament met. Eagerness for war. Cranfield impeached.

1625   January, Mansfeld's expedition.

March, James I died.

May, Charles married Henrietta Maria, recusancy laws relaxed.

June, first parliament of Charles's reign met. Refused to grant tonnage and poundage for more than one year.

August, attacks on Buckingham led to parliament's
dissolution.

October, disastrous expedition to Cadiz.

1626   Promotion of Arminians in the Church began. York House
Conference failed to resolve differences. Religion henceforth
a major issue in every parliament.

February, Second Parliament met. Attempt to impeach
Buckingham led to abrupt dissolution. King had no money.

October, second expedition to Spain failed even to reach the
coast.

1627   Forced loan aroused serious opposition. Five Knights' case.

June, war against France - expedition to Rhé.

1628   March, Third Parliament met. Granted Charles five subsidies
then produced the Petition of Right.

August, Buckingham assassinated.

September, Expedition to La Rochelle.

1629   January-March, second session of parliament. Ended by
Eliot's three resolutions. Charles decided to dispense with
parliament.

1629-40 The personal rule.

1629   April, peace made with France in the treaty of Suza.

1630   November, treaty of Madrid with Spain. Birth of Charles,
Prince of Wales.

1630-40 Attempt to impose Arminian practise on the country.

1632   Sir Thomas Wentworth became Lord Deputy of Ireland.

1633   William Laud became Archbishop of Canterbury. Charles
went to Scotland for the first time to be crowned. He was
accompanied by Laud.

1634   First imposition of ship money. Then levied annually up to
1640.

1637   June, trial of Prynne, Burton and Bastwick in Star Chamber.

July, riot in St Giles' Cathedral, Edinburgh on the introduction of a new prayer book.

November, Hampden's case. Only seven out of twelve judges
upheld the tax.

1638   The Covenant gained support throughout Scotland.

1639   First Bishops' War. Army assembled to fight the Scots was
unfit to fight.

June, treaty of Berwick.

1640   April, Short Parliament met and was then dissolved.

May, new canons for the Church were produced including
the 'etcetera' oath.

July, Second Bishops' War. The Scots invaded Northumberland.

October, truce agreed at Ripon.

4 November, the Long Parliament opened.

Further Reading

There is a huge volume of material on the early seventeeth century and this section can only point you in the direction of a few volumes that will be of interest. Books are being produced almost continuously and a list of recommendations such as this runs the risk of becoming out of date almost before it is printed. The following are reliable historians whose work is always worth considering - Robert Ashton, Richard Cust, Christopher Hill, Ann Hughes, Roger Lockyer, John Morrill, Conrad Russell, Kevin Sharpe.

1 Textbooks

Textbooks fall into two categories. There are staightforward chronologies and there are books of essays on specific topics. The most recent and most comprehensive of the narratives is

Roger Lockyer, *The Early Stuarts* (Longman 1989). This looks in detail at the reigns of James I and Charles I from 1603 to 1642. It is easy to read and has a detailed table of contents so that finding relevant information is not difficult. The only drawback to the book lies in the way it has been divided into chapters so that there is much cross referencing which can be off-putting.

Another chronology, which is less detailed than Lockyer but which provides a different perspective, is

Derek Hirst, *Authority and Conflict England 1603-1658* (Edward Arnold 1986).

There are a number of collections of essays on the early seventeenth century. Three of the most important are part of the Macmillan Problems in Focus series. These are

A.G.R. Smith (ed.), *The Reign of James VI and I* (Macmillan 1973) - especially the essays by Smith and Prestwich.

Conrad Russell (ed.), *The Origins of the English Civil War* (Macmillan 1973) - especially the essays by Russell, Hawkins and Tyacke.

Howard Tomlinson (ed.), *Before the English Civil War* (Macmillan 1983). This is a particularly useful book and every essay is worth careful reading.

2 Biographies

There is no satisfactory biography of James I. An impression of him can be gained from the detailed and sympathetic biography of Buckingham,

Roger Lockyer, *Buckingham: The Life and Political Career of George Villiers, First Duke of Buckingham 1592-1628* (Longman 1981).

Charles I has fared slightly better than his father but there is no outstanding biography of him. A straightforward account is given in

Charles Carlton, *Charles I: the Personal Monarch* (Routledge and Kegan Paul 1983).

3 Specialist Studies

There are a huge variety of these and it is likely that your local library will have its own method of selection. Do not worry if you are unable to obtain the titles listed below. They represent some of the accessible work on the period which has appeared in recent years, but they are in no sense compulsory reading.

R. Cust and A. Hughes (eds.), *Conflict in Early Stuart England, Studies in Religion and Politics 1603-1642* (Longman 1982).

This is a useful collection of post-revisionist essays. Especially recommended are the introduction and the essays by Lake, Cogswell and Thompson.

There are two books which take as their starting point the causes of the civil war but they have much of interest to say on the earlier period.

Ann Hughes, *The Causes of the English Civil War* (Macmillan 1991).

This interesting book puts the civil war in its British and European setting. It is relatively easy to read and would repay careful study once you have mastered the shape of the period. It is not a book to tackle first but could profitably be used in conjunction with Lockyer or Hirst.

Conrad Russell, *The Causes of the English Civil War* (O.U.P. 1990).

Confusingly sharing the same title as the Hughes book, this provides a stimulating contrast to it. This book was originally a series of lectures and it is written in a colloquial style which is easy to understand. Russell is the senior revisionist and Hughes represents the younger post-revisionists. Reading the two books together gives an opportunity to compare the two points of view.

Kevin Sharpe, *The Personal Rule of Charles I* (Yale 1992).

This is a magnificent book, controversial, well-written, generously illustrated and handsomely produced. However, it is not to be undertaken lightly because it is 950 pages long! It is possible to dip into it using the comprehensive index, and the sections on the Church and on foreign policy make particularly stimulating reading. The first section provides a summary of Charles I's reign up to 1629 that is well worth reading even if the rest of the book seems too daunting.

4 Sources on The Early Stuarts 1603-40

If it is at all possible, a visit to the National Portrait Gallery in London is to be recommended. It makes the history of the period come to life if you can look at the faces of those involved. There are a number of compilations of source extracts. Four of the most easily obtainable are:

Robert Ashton, *James I by his Contemporaries* (Hutchinson 1969);

J.P. Kenyon (ed.), *The Stuart Constitution 1603-88* 2nd edition (C.U.P. 1986);

C.W. Daniels and J.S. Morrill, *Charles I* (C.U.P. 1988);

Ann Hughes (ed), *Seventeenth Century England A Changing Culture 1 Primary Sources* (Ward Lock Educational 1980).

Index

Readers seeking a specfic piece of information might find it helpful to consult the table of *Contents* and the *Chronological Table* as well as this brief *Index*.